COWBOYS

The Real Story of Cowboys and Cattlemen

COWBOYS

The Real Story of Cowboys and Cattlemen

Royal B. Hassrick

First published in paperback in the
United States of America 1975 by
Derbibooks and distributed by
Book Sales Inc., 110 Enterprise Avenue
Secaucus, N.J. 07094

© 1974 Octopus Books Limited

ISBN 0 7064 0487 4

Produced by Mandarin Publishers Limited
Toppan Building, Westlands Road, Quarry Bay,
Hong Kong

Printed in Hong Kong

Contents

Introduction

The rugged nature of the country and the harshness of the climate presented the cowboy with any number of difficulties.
Bottom: *Cattle grazing in Jemez Canyon, New Mexico.* Left: *Relic of an old plank road across the desert between Yuma, Arizona, and El Centro, California*

Of all American culture heroes, the cowboy stands head and shoulders above the others. The purpose of this book is to tell about these men and their way of life as well as to describe something of the history of America's dramatic cattle industry.

The significance of the early Spanish *rancheros* to the later cowboy culture is a unique contribution. Many of the words, trappings and methods of handling stock owe their origin to the *vaqueros* and *caballeros* of Texas and the great Southwest. Words like lariat from *la reata*, lasso from *lazo reata*, cavvy from *caballado*, a 'bunch of horses' and many more are firmly established in cowboy lingo. Colorful as the *vaquero* was, the Spanish, with the exception of a hide and tallow trade in California, were never truly in the beef business.

It was only after the Civil War that the true cowboy evolved. The importance of beef to a burgeoning population in the East added an incentive to what had been a desultory sort of cattle gathering. While it all began in Texas with the great cattle drives, the cowboy's territory spread from Kansas north to Canada and west from Arizona and Nevada to Utah and Idaho. The regions of the Great Plains, the Rocky Mountains and the Great Basin and Plateau varied in terrain and climate, but the essential and common requirement was grass.

The western parts of the Dakotas, Kansas, Oklahoma and Texas and the eastern reaches of New Mexico, Colorado, Wyoming and Montana

were rich in highly nutritious grasses. These were the Plains, the area which had supported the vast herds of buffalo. By its nature, it now became ideal for grazing cattle. It was a country, however, subject to dry and searing heat in the summers and frigid, windswept blizzards in the winter. The undulating and unending sea of grass possessed a monotony that tried the spirit. It was in this treeless vastness that 'a man could look farther and see less' than any place in the Nation.

The Rocky Mountains, including parts of Colorado, Wyoming and Montana possessed lush valleys, but suffered hard winters. The majesty of the country, while handsome to behold, was harsh and cruel with unbelievably deep snows making life for the cowboy and his cows a matter of survival of the toughest.

In the Great Basin and Plateau regions of Nevada, Utah and Idaho the grass was sparse. The same was true of southwest Texas, New Mexico

Below: *A wagon train is attacked by Indians, just one of the many dangers facing migrants going West.* Right: *Cattle grazing near the ghost town of Bodie, California*

One of the most celebrated cowboys of movie fame,
John Wayne has appeared in countless films
depicting life in the West

and much of Arizona. In the Great Plains a rancher could plan to run a cow to every ten acres. In the far West, because of its barren and arid character, much more land was required to support one animal. The heat of summer here, the scarcity of water, the tremendous distances between ranches and settlements made the work of tending cattle arduous and lonesome. But in no locality was cowboying ever meant to be easy. The rugged character of the region made for rugged men.

The roughness of the country and the nature of the work called for men of fortitude and endurance. It has been the object of this book to show cowboy life as it really was. The cowboy has been described as stoic and taciturn, and that he was. The lonesomeness of the job predestined it, for he spent many hours alone in the saddle with no one to communicate with but himself. And yet, when cowboys got together, they carried on a rough sort

As the Easterners took their families West in search of a new life the townships grew and so did the amenities, stores, hotels, saloons and inevitably gambling houses. Above: *The Stone Hotel in Oklahoma offered more than just a bed. Below: A town on the plains*

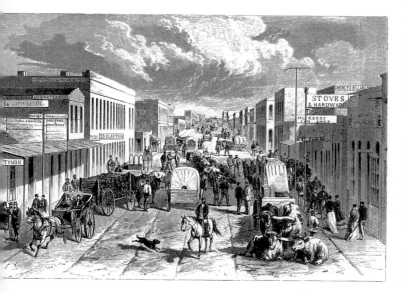

of camaraderie, a crude kind of bantering and practical jokes of the hardest nature that not only made the job bearable, but lightened it with a brand of humor which is found to this day.

There's the story of a rancher whose newborn calves were being decimated by an especially virulent scourge known as 'scours'. The veterinarian was called in. While he prescribed preventative medication, he also strongly urged burying the little victims in hopes of reducing contamination. 'Well,' said Dallas as he looked on, 'you didn't think we were so dumb as to bury the live ones.'

Not all cowboying today is simply a matter of riding the range on 'Old Paint'. The horseman must also undertake such mundane chores as baling hay, cleaning out the hen house, even plowing. The following anecdote illustrates the cowpuncher's flair for making jokes out of the monotony of his work.

It was a bitterly cold autumn day when Buck bundled himself in a green waffled parka, elk hide gloves and a brand new, fake fur, ear-flapped cap.

Astride a huge diesel tractor, he and Tex dragged their pair of four gang plows ' 'round and 'round' the hundred acre field. After about an hour or so, a little twister or whirlwind attacked Buck, blowing off his fake fur hat. He quickly pulled to a stop, only to see his new hat plowed into a furrow. Climbing off his monstrous machine, he ran back and began to dig into the earth, hoping to retrieve his new purchase. Just then Tex arrived, stopped his rig and yelled, 'Hey, Buck, lookin' for gold?'

'Hell no, I just plowed under my new cap and damn if I can find it.'

'Don't worry,' barked Tex, 'just wait till Spring and you'll have a whole crop of little ones.'

This book is written with the clear knowledge that the library shelves are already filled with a host of books on the subject. The little card files in the neat drawers take up many inches of literature on the topic. I even came across a title listed as *Cowboys Don't Cry*. Right then and there I had my doubts as to whether the author had ever punched

Above: *Interior of a settler's cabin.* Below: *Annie Oakley, one of the best-known cowgirls of the West*

Left: 'Big Brass Buckle and Baggy Blue Jeans', the standard uniform of every hardworking cowboy. His style of dress is imposed on him by the rigors of the job such as driving cattle across a river (right). Below left: Cemetery in Tombstone, Arizona. In the days of the pioneers justice was not always fair

cows, but I did know that the writer had caught something of the character, the backbone of what makes for the American culture hero.

I've never seen a cowboy weep wet tears. It's too dry in the West to permit that sort of thing to happen. But any cowman worth his salt, who has had to shoot his horse because it broke its leg, or has seen his calves die like flies from scours, or seen the price drop just when he must sell his calf crop to pay the bills, will undoubtedly come near to tears. To be thrown from a horse and have your sternum torn apart, to be gored by a maddened cow and be on a crutch for three weeks, to have your face torn apart by flying parts of a broken machine, could bring some people to tears; but not the cowboy. I guess they're kind of numb.

This book has been written because, as a former rancher, I thought it well worth recording something of the history and something of the present-day activities of the cattle industry. It has been my observation that in the many, many books about cowboys and especially in the movies, particularly those shown on the TV series, few described the essential whys of the cow business. Scene after scene show cowboys chasing rustlers, breaking broncos, shooting up the town or brawling in a saloon and dying of 'lead poisoning', all of which occurred. But to see cowhands branding whereat no smoke appears or to observe no dickering when cows are sold at the end of the trail drive is strange to me. These omissions and others like them may have some purpose in fictionalizing the story of the cowboy, but they evade the realities of the cattle business. This book endeavors, as they say, to tell it like it is.

Then, too, the deluge of 'Westerns', the books, the movies and the TV shows with which the public is swamped, are almost invariably presented in the past tense as historical novels. Very seldom is anything written or shown about the contemporary scene. As a cowboy I was impressed by how very much of cowboy culture actually has been retained, and in fact exists today. At the end of a day's work, whether mending a fence, pulling a cow from a mud hole or baling hay, I would often relate

Above: *The 'Prairie Schooner', an emigrant wagon crossing the plains.* Below: The Magic of the Drop *by Frederic Remington*

some humorous situation that had taken place. At length my wife insisted that I should record these ridiculous matters. She pointed out that the life of the cowboy had not died with the great cattle drives nor the big Wyoming cow spreads of the late nineteenth century. As a result, I began to make notes of daily happenings. Some of these little narratives appear in this book, partly with the object of showing that the cowboy is still very much alive, partly with the purpose of explaining the factual aspects of contemporary ranching.

This is not a 'How To Do It' book. Because of their popularity, it was tempting to write such a dissertation. There are, however, many extremely good ones on the market and their scope is amazing, from how to train a horse to how to operate a ranch. At best, these books are dullish and become sparkling only if the reader is inspired with the urge to become a cowboy. Then they become the textbook and the Bible. I mention this because there are some people who think this a good way of life. The point is, there is plenty of sound literature on the topic. However, all the hours and hours of reading and study cannot make a cowboy. No book, no matter how descriptively written, can tell a man how to sit a horse or how to brand a calf. Only by

Above: *Cowboys do not always see eye to eye.* A row in a cattle town *by Remington*

Below: '*A Cowboy's Holiday*': *leisure time would be spent in the saloons and gambling halls*

The nature of the cowboy's daily chores meant that he was compelled to spend many hours alone in the saddle. As a result he generally gained the reputation of being stoic and taciturn

actually doing the job can that be accomplished and the best way to learn the techniques is to hire out to a rancher as a cowhand.

The successful rancher has always been an astute businessman. Armed with a good knowledge of the economics of the business, he gambled against the odds of the elements, of disease and sudden death, of thieves and rustlers and of a fluctuating and more often unpredictable market. His employees were his cowhands, a motley lot of hard-working, hard-living and often soft-hearted men. It was they who would care for a stranded calf with more compassion than a female Salvation Army officer could succor a drunken bum on a blizzardy Christmas Eve.

It is worthwhile to note that these very cowboys, pictured as Westerners par excellence, were in reality, as often as not, transplanted Easterners. Records show in the 1880s and 1890s that young men as far east as Virginia, Pennsylvania and New York ventured 'West'. They must have been enamored by the terribly rough, he-man way of life. I can attest to it. I was born in New Jersey.

The cowboy is a man of few words, often succinct and more often rough. His statements are frequently punctuated with so many 'damnits' and 'oh hells' that one must listen carefully to get the gist of the sentence. Sometimes, however, one can get the idea pretty quickly. When a horse steps on a cowboy's toe, he does not say 'Please, dear horse, remove your foot from my boot. You're hurting my toe and spoiling the shine.' Rather, he very simply yells, 'Get the hell off my foot, you son-of-a-bitch.'

DICK JOHNSON.

LILLIAN F. SMITH.

ANNIE OAKLEY.

GABRIEL DUMONT.

CARTER COUTRIER.

W. F. CODY.

YOUNG CHIEF.

JIM MITCHELL.

JOHN M. BURKE.

NATE SALSBURY.

BUCK TAYLOR.

Cowboys were acknowledged as hard drinkers. 'Sour mash', a corn liquor, was their favorite, partly because that was really all that was available. When they came to town, the saloon became their club. If they weren't gambling at their popular card game of faro, they lounged at the bar telling tall tales. Some yarns were universal. Every cow-puncher has had to listen to them time and again and laughs raucously, just to be polite. Such is the story of the young bull and the old bull standing on a ridge. Below them was a lush valley where twenty cows peacefully grazed. 'Say,' said the young bull, 'why don't you and I run down this hill and each of us make love to one of those heifers?'

'No,' replied the old bull, 'we'll walk down the hill and each make love to all of them.'

Introductions are something like footnotes. They should either be included in the text, or left out. This introduction, however, seems important, if only to tell something of the reason for writing about cowboys together with the chance to record something of the present-day scene and *raison d'être* of ranching.

In this introduction I have devoted a considerable part to cowboy humor. I think this is essential, and not because the cowboy was in any way trying to be amusing or thought himself a funny man. Rather, because his life was so deprived of any amenities, he was skillfully able to make the best of a hard bargain and, to his credit, find fun in life. Adversity was his daily meal and maybe that's the secret.

Books aren't written by one man alone and this is no exception. Many writers of the West have described the cowboy's role and artists have delineated his way of life. Some of these men were cowmen themselves and this book is indebted to their observations and insights. As important, however, as these sources were, the cowboys and cattlemen with whom I worked were indeed the most helpful of all.

"DANCE HIGHER — DANCE FASTER."

Old-Time Cowboys and Big Cattle Drives

The story of the cowboy is a tale filled with romance. The truth is, however, that little real romance exists; it is simply a saga of courageous men who don't know they are brave. It is the history of the American cattle industry in all its ramifications, and it is filled with adventure and drama, with ambition and harsh justice. No one group of men holds such a fascination for so many as do these bold horsemen. Their daring and fortitude, their stoicism and loyalty, their taciturn demeanor combined with boisterous exuberance, give them a charisma enjoyed by few other men. They are the American folk heroes and their pre-eminence is unmatched.

They are usually represented as being Indian fighters, and it is true that, upon occasion, they were. But their skirmishes with Indians were incidental. Unlike the United States cavalry protecting the pioneers, the cowboys and Indians never waged war.

The cowboy as a dashing and colorful character took shape from the ashes of that horrible conflagration—the Civil War. But long before this there were men whose job it was to tend cattle. Christopher Columbus first brought livestock to the New World on his second voyage, but it took one Gregorio de Villalobos in 1521 to bring beef on the hoof from Santo Domingo to the mainland. It is recorded that he carried seven hardy Spanish Andalusian calves, six heifers and one young bull.

As the years passed and the Spanish control of Mexico spread northward, so did the cattle. Spanish hidalgos received grants of land, extensive grants, grants always and necessarily along the sparse water-courses or close to the far-spread, oasis-like springs of the great Southwest. In company with the landowners, the Franciscan friars established missions, eventually as far north as San Francisco, as far east as San Antonio. And with them the hidalgos and the friars brought their livestock, sheep and goats, horses and cattle. To mind the cattle, the Spaniards taught their Indian slaves and peons to ride their tough Spanish horses.

By 1750, not only had these little Mexican Indians been taught to ride horses and tend cattle, but they had been invested with all the accouterments of the Spanish horseman. Tooled leather chaparajos protected their legs against the cactus and mesquite. Wide-brimmed sombreros guarded their heads against the sun. High-pommeled and cantled saddles were patterned after a medieval predecessor. Even their cruel spurs were Spanish, though they might wear them barefooted or at best over a pair of sandals. They carried a lariat, which could be employed both as weapon and tool.

These were the vaqueros and their work was hard and lonely. They set their camp—crude lean-to-style shelters of sticks and rawhide—at a desolate water-hole, often many miles from the hacienda. Their diet was principally corn mush and wild game. The Southwest was a barren, desolate country of unbelievable beauty and grandeur, inhabited by the solitary stalking mountain lion, bands of vicious 'javalinas' or peccaries, the prairie wolf and the stealthy 'tigre' or jaguar. Worse still were the marauding bands of Apache, Comanche and later Kiowa Indians. But it was also a bounteous country, rich in deer and antelope, wild turkey and jack rabbits. To defend themselves, and to capture their food supply, the vaqueros had only a bow and arrow and they needed nothing more; they were experts.

While the lonesome vaquero minded his master's cattle, the hidalgo in his established hacienda managed a small agricultural empire. From what is now California to Texas, the ranchos spread. Some were modest adobe dwellings surrounded by crude corrals and simple sheds, others were imposing structures with handsomely carved portals and decorated vegas, cooled by the very thickness of

Indians attack and cowboys run for cover, in A Dash for Timber *by Frederic Remington*

Encroachment by the white man was resisted valiantly by the American Indians. Often the white men they would see most conspicuously advancing into their territory would be the vaqueros at their lonely work, and the ensuing struggles were frequently fatal to horses as well as men. An Episode in the Opening up of the Cattle Country by Frederic Remington

the pristine, white-plastered walls. Such a ranchero, living amidst the elegance of richly carved furnishing and lavish silver, was himself a striking figure. From his embroidered sombrero to his silver spurs, he was a match for any Spanish grandee.

No matter how vigilant the vaquero might be, how loyal to his master he was, cows and even horses wandered and strayed. What inevitably happened, from the time Cortez first brought horses to the continent and de Villalobos introduced cows, was that here and there a couple of horses or a half-dozen cows strayed and became lost in the rugged barrens of the endless wasteland of the Southwest; and, adding to the problem, rapacious Indians were ever lurking to capture a herd of horses or steal a beef.

To help insure an owner's property right, the Spanish utilized a method which they deemed most time-tested; burning into the flesh an indelible mark. Cortez asserted his rights by branding a G on the cheek of his Indian slaves. As a Christian bigot, he marked his cattle with three crosses †††, undoubtedly to symbolize the Father, the Son and the Holy Ghost. God help the man who would dare transgress this sacred sign. As Cortez had identified his livestock, so did the hidalgo make his mark. And thus it was that branding became the established method of identification for all men who tended cattle and herded horses.

Oddly, it was the strays themselves which added a singular impetus to the future of the cattle industry. Little herds of wild cattle roamed here and there through the dense mesquite pastures, grazed in hidden arroyos in the land of great mesas. And in this barren, empty wasteland they multiplied. From the original Andalusian stock emerged a hardy, rugged animal possessed of great stamina, an ability to survive with little water and sometimes on meager feed. Surprisingly, these animals acquired two unique features—great size and tremendous horns, an attribute which gave them their name, the Texas Longhorn. There has been no beast quite like it before or since.

Much as the Longhorn evolved, so did the cow pony. Both Cortez and Coronado took horses on

their expeditions—small horses of Arabian breeding. It is believed that strays from these herds, as well as animals wandering from the great Mexican haciendas, were the progenitors of the western mustang.

These wild horses thrived, and by adapting to the wild desert conditions of the Southwest, they prospered. Like the Longhorns, they too became a tough breed. But instead of attaining size, they acquired a stamina unparalleled by any horse. For sheer speed, orneriness, endurance and headstrong brains, no animal could outdistance or outsmart the mustang. No animal except man. And even for him it was a deuce of a hard job.

The mustang was a small, wiry, close-coupled horse. The Indians (probably the Comanches first, then the more northerly tribes such as the Utes and Shoshoni, and later the Sioux and Crow) captured and broke them; and it was these Plains Indians who earned the reputation as the world's greatest horsemen. The vaqueros, and later the cowboys

Above: Wild Horses *by George Catlin.* Right: *James Walker's* Vaqueros Roping a Bear *shows Spanish origins of cowboy's equipment*

as well, likewise captured the mustangs and broke them to work cattle. Some became manageable and their stamina and speed proved them invaluable. Others were utterly recalcitrant and as broncos were a difficult nuisance in any ranchero's remuda.

The settling of the Southwest by the Spanish with missions and ranchos sparsely scattered here and there in the deserts' vastness, was nonetheless a reality by the end of the eighteenth century. And a short while afterwards the United States began to show interest in this unknown region.

As early as 1800 Philip Nolan made an expedition to capture wild horses as far west as the Brazos River. It was an absolute fiasco. He was attacked by Spanish troops and killed for his efforts. In 1806 Zebulon Pike was sent on an exploring expedition to the land that was to become Texas. Though the word was probably never put in writing, his

mission was a spying operation, pure and simple. By 1820, Moses Austin, a Yankee from Connecticut, was able to convince the Spanish authorities in San Antonio of an enterprising colonization scheme. Austin died before his plan materialized but his son, Stephen, carried on and in 1822 some 150 settlers had been enlisted.

The Revolution of 1821 freed Mexico from Spanish domination and the new government was at once anxious to develop its country. Settlers paid taxes, found a market for their cattle and cattle products and even scented a chance of prosperity. Not only were American settlers given sizeable grants, but individuals and families, men from Kentucky and Tennessee, were offered either 177 acres for farming or 4,428 acres for grazing. The shrewd Americans quite naturally accepted the grazing grants. By 1835, it was estimated that the American population had reached 35,000; and among that population were the forefathers of the American cowboy, for already many of the men, rather than grub at growing cotton, were raising cattle. The stage was now set for the birth of the cowboy culture—and a culture it surely was.

In 1848, there were, according to tax records, over 350,000 cattle in Texas and by 1855 there were over a million, not counting the wild ones. With so many cattle, markets had to be found. Men who were sufficiently astute did just that.

As early as 1846, Edward Piper, anxious to find an outlet for his cows, drove a herd to Ohio, where he sold them at a profit. Another man, W. H. Snyder, lured by the thought that he could get rich from the California goldminers' strikes of 1849, drove cattle from Texas to San Francisco. It took him and his men two years. Unfortunately, he kept no records, so no one will ever know how he made out financially, if at all. At least he didn't try it again.

In 1855 some enterprising cowboys drove a herd of semi-wild Longhorns all the way to New York City. Like Snyder, they made no report.

At the conclusion of the costly Civil War, the South was an economic shambles and Texas was no exception. Returning soldiers found their farms in ruins, their livestock strayed. However, these far-seeing soldiers soon realized that a growing demand for meat in the burgeoning Northeast could prove an economic boon. Not only were railroad tycoons boldly stretching their tracks toward the great plains, but the development of the meat-packing houses were instrumental in getting beef to the eastern urban centers. These factors, combined with the introduction of ice-packed boxcars and the invention of the 'airtight' or tin can, gave impetus to the entire industry.

There was no such thing as a typical cattle drive —no two were just alike, nor could they be. Weather conditions, number of cows, caliber and experience of the drovers, the ever-present threat of Indian attack, even the market price of cattle at the end of the trail, each factor contributed to the vagaries of success or failure.

Ike Pryor, an ardent organizer and drover, figured that an efficient drive involved about three thousand head of Longhorns, one trail boss or 'ramrod,'

Left: Longhorn Cattle Drive in the 1870s. Below: A gallery of so-called 'cattle kings,' men whose wealth was counted by the head, earned by the risky hard work of their cowboy employees

Jared L. Brush.

Charles Lux.

R. G. Head.

John H. Iliff.

Thos. H. Lawrence.

John W. Snyder.

John T. Lytle.

CATTLE KINGS.

Four pictures by Charles M. Russell, one of the finest painters of Western scenes, particularly for his portrayals of the swift physical action that characterized much of the cowboys' day-to-day labor
This page: *Cowboys roping steers, and bringing them in, during a roundup.* Right: Wild Horse Hunters. Below: *In the 1890s, a group of Texas cowhands face the photographer armed with revolvers and Winchester rifles*

nine men, a cook and between 60 and 66 horses. He expected to pay his trail boss $100 a month; his cook $50 at most, plus all he could eat, and nine cowboys $30 per month. His provisions would cost $300, based on a three-month drive. Another way of calculating his expenses was to reckon a cost of about a dollar a head per mile to drive cattle. He calculated that by paying $8 per head, selling at the railhead (perhaps Abilene or Dodge City) for $20, and by subtracting his expenses and losses through death, strays and stolen stock, he could realize a profit of $30,000. A drover could get rich on a single drive if he didn't lose everything in a stampede, a flooding river, a blizzard or a dried-up market at the railhead.

The organizer of a drive was a daring entrepreneur. It took a man with a will to gamble, with stamina and guts, with determination and courage to drive a herd of half-wild cattle over 3,000 miles, across rugged and barren land that stretched from southern Texas to central Kansas.

A Texas cattleman might decide to drive his own herd north to the mecca of the railheads, but

31

more commonly a drover would buy cattle from several herds at a given price. He himself would then assume the financial risk with the hope of great profit.

Under such an arrangement, the cattle were rounded up and collected at an agreed starting point. Each owner sent out his cowboys to gather the cattle.

Collecting the cows, often at a public corral, first involved gathering them. Getting them out of the dense thickets was an almost impossible job. It meant not only knowing where they might be hidden, but also driving them through the mass of tangled underbrush that was often nothing but a maze of trails hidden by thorny bushes and prickly plant life. This was tough, hard work and the wild cows were quick and anything but co-operative. For that type of animal, roping was often the only method of securing them. The Texans carried especially short lariats, rarely more than 30 feet long, for a snare of greater length would only tangle in the mesquite and chaparral.

As the cows were assembled—and all cattle, whether cow or calf, heifer or steer, even bulls, were referred to as 'cows'—they were sorted for ownership according to their brands. There was no selection for quality, the cows were all about the same. Each was a rangy, lanky, gaunt mass of beef and hide with a fabulous set of horns.

Despite the Longhorn's great size, he was thin-fleshed, lanky and slow to mature. His size did not equate with quality. His horns, sometimes measuring over seven feet from tip to tip, though possibly advantageous in self-defense, were a distinct handicap when it came to shipping. In a crowded boxcar, these sharp-pointed stilettos were a severe hazard to every other animal, for they tore up the hides, bruised the muscles and reduced the overall value of the carcass.

His ability to range, however, was phenomenal.

Without concern, a steer would graze as much as fifteen miles from water and go without drinking for over forty-eight hours. On cattle drives, Longhorns were known to go without water for as much as four days and nights. This characteristic, combined with an inbred ability to withstand heat, to sustain themselves on the most barren of land and to remain immune to the ravages of tick fever, made the Longhorn an important asset.

The term 'beef' or 'beeves' was applied to any animal over four years old and it was worth from three dollars to eight dollars at the roundup. All cattle were bought and sold by the head, not by weight.

In gathering the cows, it was only natural that many would be found to be without brands. These were known as 'mavericks' and the determination of ownership was absolutely impossible.

There are several versions as to how the term 'maverick' came to be applied to unbranded cattle, but one, which seems most logical, will suffice. One Samuel A. Maverick, a colonel and practicing attorney in San Antonio in 1845 received as a fee, not cash, but one hundred Longhorn cows. These animals were unbranded, nor did the colonel bother to see to it that his slaves put his mark on them.

There is reason to believe the lawyer didn't even have a brand. There are plenty of records of lawyers who didn't have sense enough to make a will, and Maverick likely falls into that category.

At any rate, sometime later, as his herd multiplied, an interested buyer named Toutant Beauregard was quick to discover the cows were unmarked and forthwith claimed Maverick's cattle and all other unbranded animals for his own, branding them with his sign.

The term 'maverick' is still used today for any unmarked yearling or a calf that won't stay with its mother.

The general agreement among stockmen with respect to 'mavericks' was that during the roundup, the unmarked animals would be divided up, each man getting a fair share. Different rules applied at different times and in different periods; sometimes it was a pro-rata basis depending on how many cows each owner was known to possess, sometimes it was an accepted fact that an enterprising cowboy could build a herd by putting his brand on any unmarked cow he could find. Many a Texas ranch started just that way, but many a freelance Texas cowboy, tempted by the opportunity of establishing title to a free cow, lost his life at the point of a .45. Two men claiming the same cow spelled nothing less than trouble and sometimes death.

When the roundup was completed and the cattle belonging to the various owners were sorted and counted, the buyer or drover received a bill of sale from each rancher for the cattle sold. With the exception of the mavericks, each cow carried the brand of its owner, but in releasing them to the buyer, all the cows were given a 'vent' brand or 'road' brand, a kind of additional bill of sale indicating the buyer as a 'vendor' of the cattle in his charge. Some animals, which might have passed through three or four owners, were literally covered with brands.

In starting a drive, it was customary to push the cows hard for the first twenty-five or thirty miles, though some claim it was as much as one hundred miles. Men had learned that by tiring the cattle there was far less chance of the 'coasters' turning

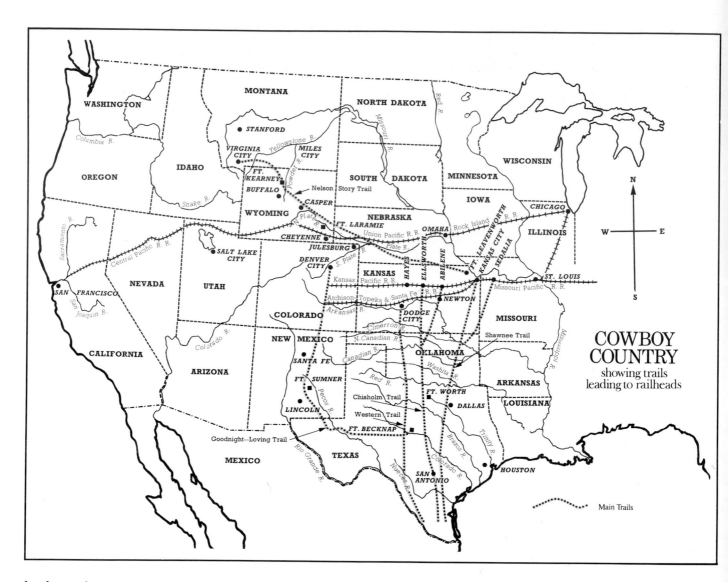

COWBOY
COUNTRY
showing trails
leading to railheads

back to the range they knew. By sundown, the cattle would be pretty tired out and no matter how strong their homing instinct might be, sheer exhaustion took command.

In a well-planned drive two 'point riders,' men most experienced in cattle driving, led the herd. At intervals along the main body rode the 'line riders' while at the rear, pushing and coaxing the lazy cows ahead amid a dense cloud of dust, were the greenhorns, inexperienced cowpunchers equipped with nothing more than a loud 'halloo' and a half-broke mustang to push the beasts along.

The first few days of a drive were especially difficult. The cows, particularly the young steers, were upset and nervous, ready to bolt at any opportunity. Some men made a point of including in their herd three or four old bulls. They found that the bulls' status and sobriety helped calm the herd and offset the antics of the exuberant young steers.

At dusk, when it became time to bed the cattle down, wise and fortunate was the drover who staked out a suitable watering place. Here the cows could drink, rest and, hopefully, sleep through the night.

The extra horses, too, had to be settled. Usually

Enjoying cookies from the chuck wagon

two 'horse wranglers' were assigned to drive and herd the extra mounts, referred to as the 'remuda.' A rope corral was set up at each stop. Sometimes the men themselves served as temporary fence-posts until the horses were calmed down and the single rope could be tied to improvised posts and to the wheel of the chuck wagon. Occasionally, the horses were hobbled, but strangely, the single strand of rope was a line beyond which the horses would not pass.

Now the cook or 'cookie,' sometimes referred to as the 'Old Lady' or 'cossie,' would prepare the meal of baked beans, bacon, hard biscuits and rank coffee from the back of the chuck wagon. He had been hired solely for his ability to drive a team of horses, not for his culinary accomplishments. More often than not he was a dark-skinned Portuguese or an Hispano hard on his luck. Otherwise, he would never have hired out for the job. In addition to his pots and pans, his equipment included one shovel, for his responsibilities included not only feeding the men, but burying the dead. The one attribute that 'cookie' did not possess, according to

any cowboy ever questioned about the matter, was an ability to cook!

'Hey, come and get it!' or 'Grub pile!' was the call to which every man on the drive responded.

Beans, bacon and coffee might not be much, but that was the fare. One cowboy, so upset at the rotten quality of the mess, in a fit of rage, shot dead the cook. The other cowboys, realizing they might starve as a result of his rashness, planned to lynch the murderer. But the drover intervened, and with a Solomon-like decision ordered that the killer should forthwith become 'cookie' for the remainder of the drive. The meals were even worse than before.

The night-herders, men responsible for watching the cows, would select from the remuda a horse for the task. The men were given shifts, sometimes four hours, usually two. The job of night-herder was no easy one and demanded that the cattle be constantly watched lest they become 'spooked' and stampede.

The least unexpected noise—the yipping of a coyote, a clap of thunder, even the mere striking of

a match—might cause one timorous steer to bolt,
whereupon the entire herd would most likely rush
off in disastrous flight. To help prevent this misfortune, the night-riders sang to the cattle—soft,
gentle, little lullabies. Some of their songs have
come down to us today, others are lost in the starlit
blackness of the great plains of bygone days. But
the legend of the singing cowboy is very real, even
to the extent that if an aspiring cowhand couldn't
sing, he very well might not get hired.

A verse from one of these songs gives an idea of
what the cowboy worried about:

'Oh, say little dogies, when will you lie down
And give up this shifting and roving around?
'My horse is leg weary, and I'm awfully tired
But if you get away, I'm sure to get fired.
Lie down, little dogies, lie down
Hi-yo, hi-yo, hi-yo.'

These sad little songs were unaccompanied by
any instrument. A guitar would have been an
impossible encumbrance on a cattle drive, and a
mouth organ would have terrified the cows. The
picture of a bunch of happy cowboys on a cattle
drive, sitting around their campfire singing to the
twang of a banjo is pure romantic balderdash.

Those cowboys who were not assigned night
watch or who drew a later shift, usually turned in
after supper. There wasn't much else to do and
twelve or more hours in the saddle induced fatigue.
There were no tents on a cattle drive. Using their
saddles as a pillow, the men rolled up in blankets
beneath the starry heavens.

Rain was particularly unpleasant. Even though
the men carried great yellow, oilskin slickers and
might use their hats as a sort of umbrella, trying
to sleep in mud and cold running water is never
really comfortable. But then when you are making
a dollar a day, you can accept some little in-
conveniences.

The mere thought of a stampede struck terror
in every cowman and while his little songs were his
best insurance, he took other precautions too. He
could intersperse his herd with tame bulls, he could
plan his drive in the early spring so that his cows
would be fat and content on the greening grass, and

he could be sure to rid himself of boisterous young steers. All too often there were one or two such animals that seemed to revel at the chance of bolting. The cowboys were alert to these recalcitrants and learned to spot them, often cutting them out of the herd, either by turning them loose or shooting them. 'Green' beef, or uncured meat, was better than bacon.

No matter how diligent the night-watchers were, no matter how earnestly they sang their lullabies, stampedes seemed inevitable. A lightning or hail storm was the frequent cause, and at the first or second crack of thunder, a steer might jump and start to bolt. Others followed and almost immediately the entire herd would be a rushing mass of pounding hooves and swinging horns.

The cowboys were more or less powerless to halt the onrush, but try they did. Every man except 'cookie' was pressed into the chase, the object being to ride amongst the leaders and try to turn the herd in upon itself, thus causing the cattle to 'mill' in a circling mass around and around until they finally came to an exhausted halt.

This was especially dangerous. Trying to get to the head of the herd often meant riding among the fast-moving cows. In the black of night the cowpony's misstep in a prairie dog hole or a hidden ravine could mean instant death by trampling.

Often the cattle would run for many miles, only to be found scattered here and there, in little bunches, all over the prairie. It was the cowhand's job to collect as many as possible, for each lost animal reduced the drover's chance of profit. Sometimes several days were spent searching for strays, but even so, many cows were often lost.

If storms were particularly severe, or the cattle especially nervous, one stampede might follow another. It was common knowledge that if a herd once bolted, it was more than likely to do so again. It is recorded that one Texas herd stampeded eighteen times in one night and that another ran over forty miles before it came to a halt.

Above: *When a cowboy removes his hat it is a sign of deep respect. These men are mourners at a fellow cowhand's funeral.* Below: Cowboy in the Rain *by Ace Powell.* Bottom: *Herding cattle in New Mexico.* Right: *Longhorns cross the Red River on a drive from San Antonio, Texas, to Dodge City, Kansas*

In addition to searching for cattle after a stampede, the men had the grim job of counting heads or reriding the trail in search of the trampled remains of a comrade. If, sadly, a mangled body should be found, the cook got down his spade. Here he dug a simple grave as the cowboys held their hats in tribute—nothing more.

The successful drover was a man of great experience and possessed of leadership ability. He knew the right trails, how far it was between water-holes and rivers, the best places to bed the cattle down. After the herd had been pushed hard the first few days, it was allowed to move at a slower pace of between twelve and fifteen miles per day. This gave the animals time to graze and fatten on the way.

No matter what trail was currently popular, from the early Shawnee to the celebrated Chisholm, each traversed many rivers—the Colorado and Brazos and Red to the south, the Canadian and Cimarron and Arkansas farther north. These rivers, albeit shallow, were often wide, and if the season had been rainy they could become raging torrents. There was not one bridge over any of them, so each must be forded.

It was considered good practice when approaching a river to keep the cattle moving, urging the lead steers to continue their pace, swimming the river to maintain the momentum. The men riding 'point' and 'flank' would swim their horses in the accustomed position to keep the cows in line. One old drover, Colonel Snyder, had two lead 'swimming steers' who were trained, more or less, to plunge into the rivers ahead of the herd and lead it across. He used these animals on drive after drive.

It was not always easy, especially if the water was high, to get the cattle started. Once having entered, swimming with their heads just out of the water,

many became caught in the swift currents. There they might be sucked under, washed downstream or drown from exhaustion. The cowboys' job was, at all costs, to prevent such a disaster.

Most dangerous was the situation where the cattle, having already started across, became frightened by a floating log or sudden change in current and began to turn back and circle upon themselves. Now the cowboys had to swim their horses among the piercing horns, yelling and yipping to try to untangle the milling cows lest they be washed downriver and drown. If a man became dismounted in the river, he would be lucky to grab his horse's tail or that of a steer and be dragged to shore. He might try swimming, but many a man was drowned. Yet with all these hardships, there is no record of a herd failing to cross a river.

The tempers of the cows and the vagaries of the elements were not the only matters which brought grief to the cowboy. When the herds had crossed the Red River, they entered Indian Territory, a vast stretch of land that was later to become Oklahoma. This was country set aside for many eastern tribes—the Cherokee, Choctaw, Chickasaw, Creeks and others. These were farming people who had crops and livestock of their own and they were dismayed and angered at the thousands of trampling hooves destroying their properties and damaging their pastures. A highly sophisticated group, they were quick to demand tolls from the drovers—sometimes as much as ten cents a head, other times a payment in beeves. The Texas drovers bitterly resented this blackmail, but were powerless to prevent it, for the Indians appeared in great numbers backed by firearms to prove their point.

As if this weren't enough, when the herds finally reached the Kansas border, they were confronted by an even more belligerent barrier—the 'grangers' and the Kansas Jay Hawkers. The grangers were small farmers lured to the West by cheap land. Self-reliant Yankees, they earned their living raising crops and keeping dairy herds. Terrified by the thought that the Texas Longhorns, which carried the dread Texas tick fever, might infect their herds, they formed armed bands and posses of vigilantes to ward off the Texas herds.

The Jay Hawkers, sometimes enlisted by the grangers, were a bunch of self-appointed, ne'er-do-well pirates. Composed entirely of bandits, they pillaged and robbed and were happy to hold up the Texans, demanding ransom, running off a herd and even killing the cowboys to prove their invincibility. Not a few Jay Hawkers, however, were left unburied on the prairie, killed by a stubborn cowboy.

As a result of these two groups, many herds were stalled below the Kansas border, often at great loss to the drovers. Good grazing land wore out and the cattle wasted away. Speculators, often in cahoots with the Jay Hawkers, made unconscionable deals which most Texans had no alternative but to accept.

Most Texans, however, are not all Texans. Nelson Story, in 1866, had purchased some 1,000 Longhorns in Fort Worth with the idea of selling them in the North, but, like so many others, found himself bottled up south of Baxter Springs, Kansas by the grangers and Jay Hawkers. Story had an idea, however, risky, but worthwhile. He had been a freighter on the Oregon Trail, had struck it rich in a Montana gold field and knew that there were some 10,000 hungry miners in the region of Virginia City. Besides, his bride lived there.

Moving his cattle west past the Kansas border guard, he circled his herd north to Fort Leavenworth. Here he outfitted a wagon train with oxen and bullwhackers and new Remington breech-loading rifles. Setting out with his herd and twenty-seven men, he pushed west along the Oregon Trail to Fort Laramie. The Bozeman Trail to the north swarmed with hostile Sioux Indians, and although Story was contemptuous, they attacked near Fort Reno, wounding two of his men with arrows and running off several of his beeves. Undaunted, Story and his men pursued the Indians, shot them up and retrieved every last cow.

When Story reached Fort Kearny, the frightened commandant, Colonel Henry Carrington, refused him passage, so imminent was Indian attack to the

EDWARD BOREIN

north. Since Carrington reserved the grass near the fort for his cavalry horses, corrals were built for the cattle within sight, but at such a distance to be of no protection.

Story would not be stopped. Under cover of darkness, he and his men drove the cattle out of the corrals. Now they traveled by night and grazed by day. One man, scouting ahead, was captured by Indians, scalped and pinned to the prairie with arrows before Story could rescue him. Two other Sioux attacks were parried, the Remington rifles being too hot for the Indians. And then, on December 9, 1866, with no further incidents, Story drove his herd into Virginia City, there to be welcomed by his wife who had ridden out to meet him.

If Nelson Story was courageous, so were Charles Goodnight and Oliver Loving.

Goodnight got the idea that a sound market for cattle might be in the Southwest where 7,000 Navaho Indians were held captive near Fort Sumner in New Mexico. The government had to feed these hungry souls and Goodnight believed he could make money fulfilling this need.

Goodnight, an experienced bushwhacker who knew the Southwest, met, by chance, Oliver Loving, recognized as a topnotch cattle drover. He once led a herd as far as Quincy, Illinois and two years later, in 1860, drove 1,000 head of cows as far west as Denver City to tap the market of the Colorado goldminers.

Together, these two men agreed to try to reach

Fort Sumner. It was a route fraught with trouble, a trail no one in his right mind would think of taking. By going south over the Staked Plain of Texas, the chance of attack by marauding Comanches would be somewhat reduced, but crossing 96 miles from the Middle Concho to the Pecos River, where there was absolutely no water at all, was preposterous.

With these obstacles well understood, Goodnight and Loving acquired 2,000 head of cattle—cows, bulls, steers, even calves. Goodnight also designed what is thought to be the first chuck wagon, this to be drawn by ten oxen.

Problems appeared early in the drive. The calves could not keep up with the beeves. At first the newborn were placed in the chuck wagon, but this didn't work at all and the 'little fellas' reluctantly had to be killed. While the men experienced no trouble from the Comanches, they got their share of misery from the 96 waterless miles. The cows at first were permitted to rest during the night, but instead of resting, they milled the entire time. It was decided that stopping was of no value and that since the cattle were going to be up, they might as well be heading in the right direction. By the third day the beeves had shrunk so badly that those which could move looked like dried hides stretched over a picket fence. Those that went down through thirst and exhaustion never rose again. The men and horses were not much better off. The water, stored in large barrels in the new chuck wagon, ran out. And then, on the morning of the fourth day, the animals scented water and with what little energy they could muster, weakly stampeded nearly twelve miles to the Pecos River. When they reached it, so dazed were they that they plunged clear across the river to the far bank before turning to drink.

Here Goodnight and Loving rested the herd, letting them fatten on the grassy banks and enjoy the life-giving water which flowed down the Pecos. Through all the horrors of the 96 miles of hell, Goodnight and Loving lost only 300 head. The remaining 1,700 cattle they drove to Fort Sumner to the starving Navaho. They sold their beef steers to the Government at eight cents a pound live weight—a real killing on the market!

Loving drove the remainder of the herd—cows, calves and bulls—north to Denver City where he made a good profit. Goodnight rode east from Fort Sumner to make arrangements for buying another herd to trail them west again. Some cowmen just aren't easy to stop and Charlie Goodnight and Oliver Loving were perfect examples.

While Story, Loving and Goodnight by-passed the Kansas border, many more drovers worried their way to the railheads through the grangers and Jay Hawkers. Tensions grew and animosities boiled, sometimes to the point where buyers and sellers could barely do business. And then, the whole matter was resolved, thanks to the ingenuity of a young Illinois cattle dealer, Joseph McCoy. In a flash of brainwork, he brilliantly solved the puzzle and put the pieces together. After many cold shoulders from railroad men and town fathers, he finally convinced the skeptical directors of the Kansas Pacific Railroad and the enthusiastic business leaders of the little town of Abilene, that the combination of a salesyard and railhead would prove profitable to all concerned. Here buyers could meet with Texas drovers to purchase the huge herds without interference by grangers, Jay Hawkers or unco-operative townsfolk. McCoy agreed to build the great holding pens and take a small commission on the shipments. He sent an agent to the Texas drovers who gladly turned their herds west. Almost overnight Abilene became a boom town. It took a little longer for McCoy to go bankrupt.

Here at Abilene was a genuine market where you made your profit or lost your shirt. Here you cashed in your wages, here was the reward for all the work, the loneliness, the danger—for this was truly the end of the trail.

Several trails led from southern Texas to the Kansas railheads. One of the earliest was the Shawnee, which terminated in Sedalia, Missouri and also St Louis, but as the railroads pushed farther west, other trails were developed. The famous Chisholm Trail led to Abilene and

Ellsworth, Kansas and later the Western Trail to Dodge City.

The cow towns of the 1860s and 1870s were a study in hypocrisy. Opportunistic men from the East, anxious to get rich quick from the growing numbers of grangers, became overnight bankers and merchants. With the coming of the Texans, hotels, glittering saloons, ornate gambling houses and gaudy brothels sprung up like mushrooms after a spring rain. The grangers, solid Scotch Presbyterians, resented the trespassing Texans with their disease-ridden cattle. The stolid bankers and merchants had mixed feelings—the money was very welcome, but the gambling, drinking and whoring were unfortunate yet necessary evils. As for the saloon proprietors and the madams, the

gamblers and the hotel keepers, the cattle drives were a bonanza.

The survivors of a cattle drive, the cowboys who hit the cow town, were anything but God-fearing men. These were men who had already ridden through the shadow of the valley of death. Abilene, Ellsworth and Dodge City were the pearly gates.

To control the pent-up exuberance of the cowboys and maintain a semblance of order in the community, the town fathers generally were pretty quick to employ the services of a 'lawman.' Almost without exception, these characters were as quick on the draw as they were short on the law. Life was pretty cheap, men shot first and asked questions later, and the sheriffs themselves operated on that basis. Wild Bill Hickok was probably the epitome of the western gunslinger. Having killed over seventy men, he helped keep law in Abilene.

There was a sort of homespun code of honor which worked after a fashion. Cheating at cards was unpardonable, drawing one's sixshooter on an unarmed man was a disgrace. Either offense could mean sudden death to the culprit at the hands of the victim or his friends. Arguments and brawls were commonplace, and shootings were the order of the day. The cow town was anything but peaceful.

So upset became the citizens of Abilene that in February, 1872, they sent a manifesto to the Texans not to bring their cattle to their town. The Texans obliged, but not entirely for unselfish motives. The railroads had moved farther west; new towns, like Ellsworth, offered better services. Quitting Abilene suited the cowboys just fine. The citizens of Abilene, realizing that they might have severed their life-line, hastily sent a second proclamation reversing their first, but it was too late.

Left: In Without Knocking *by Charles Russell shows a bit of fun that took place in Sanford, Montana in 1881.* Below: Drovers Cottage *was a plush 100-room hotel in Abilene, where 'Wild Bill' Hickok* (bottom) *was sheriff*

As a result, Abilene's boom burst like a circus balloon and the town sunk to a deserved oblivion.

Abilene's demise produced Ellsworth's boom, but as the railroad pushed west, Ellsworth died too. Now Dodge City blossomed into the new Cowboy Capital. Yet Dodge City, like its predecessors, those glittering dens of iniquity, was doomed to wither, though for a different reason. The winter of 1886 brought a most cruelly killing blizzard to the Great Plains. Thousands upon thousands of cattle were frozen to death leaving the entire industry in an absolute financial shambles. When the thaw finally came and the losses were counted, Dodge City just melted down like a snowball on a pot-bellied stove. Thereby ended the era of the fabulous Texas Longhorn drives and the legendary cow towns, each brought to a sudden eclipse not by sin, but by an over-supply of pretty white snowflakes.

Cattle Barons and the Great Spreads

Trail driving was not the cowboy's only occupation. Men like Chisum and Goodnight established permanent ranches in the Southwest. John Iliff acquired over thirty miles of Platte River frontage in Colorado and ranged his cattle for a hundred miles along the Platte, with Julesburg the center of his operations. Moneyed interests in the East, even as far as Great Britain, invested in cattle and valuable water rights, especially in Colorado, New Mexico, Wyoming and Montana. By the late 1870s the great spreads were being built and the powerful cattle barons were emerging.

Free grass was a major factor in the development of the huge ranches. The men who controlled the water were permitted, and often usurped the right, to range their cows as far as the animals could go and come for water. And with this pattern, the cowboy's role gradually changed from a drover to that of a herdsman.

In order to stock the northern ranches, cattle were driven from Texas. The famous song:

'Yipi ti ye, get along little dogies,
It's your misfortune and none of my own.
Yipi ti ye, get along little dogies,
You know Wyoming will be your new home.'

pretty well catches the flavor of these transactions. As more and more cattle filled the northern grazing lands, more cowboys were needed to tend and guard the boss man's cows. Many of the cow-punchers came from Texas, with the result that the northern cattle business was really quite southern in origin.

A ranch of a thousand square miles was by no means unusual, and while the borders were vague, they were generally agreed upon by the neighboring owners. Cattle that drifted from one rancher's land to another's were driven back and this required not only 'riding the line,' but also keeping a rough count and checking the general condition of the cows. Here and there, cabins of log or batten-board or huts of stone were set up at the perimeters which served as a station for one or two men. Life at a 'line camp' was a lonely vigil.

Without any question, a most vexing problem besetting the rancher was the influx of 'nesters' to the Great Plains. These were hardy and persistent men from the East, who hoped to grub a living for themselves and family from the soil. Some received 160 acres of land under the Homestead Act, others were outright squatters and held no legal claim to the land whatsoever. They erected little cabins, shacks or often rude houses of sod and tilled the acreage to eke out an existence. Like the grangers of Kansas, the use to which they put the land was diametrically opposed to that of the rancher. To the cowman, they were ruining the grass with plows just to make their nests. To a free-roaming horseman, these farmers on foot, wearing bib overalls, were objects of nothing but scorn. A cowboy was as different from a farmer as a hawk is from a chicken.

Matters were made worse by the invention of barbed wire by Joseph Farwell Glidden. By 1875 'sod busters' had run their fences around their gardens, their fields, even their little ranches, not only to the inconvenience of the cowmen, but also to their fury. Fencing the free grass was heresy. The enmity grew and many a nester awoke to find his fence cut, his gates dragged away, his livestock strayed.

The ranchers took decisive action to destroy the nesters. They sent their armed cowboys or their foreman and sometimes went out in person to confront the intruders. On more than one occasion they shot to kill. Their aim was pretty accurate.

Paradoxically, the cattlemen themselves were quick to see the advantage of a new invention. The barbed wire fence could do the job of the outrider and no longer would a man's cattle stray and mix among his neighbor's herd. Miles and miles of

A cowboy riding a bucking bronc, from an engraving by Frederic Remington

'drift' fences were stretched, sometimes an entire ranch was enclosed. But fencing in the Plains meant that the days of free grass were doomed. 'I tell you what ruined the West,' observed one old cowman. 'Barbed wire and bib overalls.'

If barbed wire and bib overalls angered the cattlemen, sheep disgusted them. Sheep thrived particularly well on the western ranges. Legally, sheep herders had just as much right to the free grass as did the cattlemen. But to the rancher, sheep were a menace. In order to thrive, these animals must be kept constantly on the move. Their grazing habits, different from cattle, are such that they crop the grass very close to the ground, and in the arid West this habit can endanger the plant by exposing the root system to the searing rays of the sun, thereby burning out the forage. An overgrazed prairie is a ruined prairie, and a ruined prairie means thin cattle and a low price for cows.

The scorn of the cattleman for the sheepman was based on this reasoning, but other factors contributed to his loathing. The sheep herders, often foreigners, were little men on foot with their gypsy-like carts and busy dogs allowing their fetid sheep to overgraze the cowman's country. Then too, the meat from their animals was barely fit to eat. For those rare cattlemen who demeaned themselves to request roast lamb at a hotel or cafe, the order was referred to as a 'plate of sheep.' The antagonistic attitude persists to this very day. One elderly cattleman, when offered his choice of roast beef or lamb by a thoughtful but naive hostess, remarked, 'Thanks lady, but I ate lamb once and gagged!'

The cowboy's enmity to the sheepman went beyond thoughts or words—it took the form of drastically cruel action. Arizona ranchers like Charles Goodnight set up 'dead lines' beyond which the sheep herders might not pass. And the stockmen patrolled those deadlines, shooting to kill any sheep herder who transgressed it. In the Ten Sleep country of Wyoming it was not unheard-of for cowboys to spread saltpeter over the sheep range, thus killing the 'bleaters.' More directly, however, the cowboys simply murdered the 'scab-herders' and happily shot and clubbed to death not hundreds but thousands of the stupid little beasts. In Arizona, a feud between the cattle-raising Graham family and the sheep herding Tewkesbury clan began in 1887 and ended five years later with

Above: The Outlying Camp *by Frederic Remington, which possessed few of the comforts of home.* Below: Dispute over a Cattle Brand *by the same painter*

twenty-six men shot down, bushwhacked, dry-gulched or lynched. It became known as the Tonto County War. Only when the last of the Tewksburys killed the sole remaining Graham did it end.

The strange thing is that for all his superior aggressiveness, in the long run the cowboy lost out to the lowly sheepman.

Yet the real, ever-present enemy of the cowman was not the sheepman, but the rustler. Despite the penalty—hanging by the neck until dead—these daring thieves were, and to this very day are, a ceaseless scourge. In the early days, the rustler was an individual trying to build a small herd by putting his brand on a maverick beeve, claiming a kind of innocent right of ownership. Many a great herd was built on this basis and in times past when thousands of cattle ran wild, the animals were considered 'fair game' for an enterprising cowboy. Some big operators paid their ranch-hands from two to five dollars for each maverick they branded, partly to discourage a cowboy from putting his own brand on the stray, partly to help the cowhand make some extra money. Later, the northern cattle barons agreed among themselves that the paying of commissions would cease and the cowboys would brand mavericks for the home ranch only. This held a

Barbed wire, which was a relatively new invention, brought many angry disputes. Right: *An advertisement for Glidden's barbed wire which appeared in Loving's brand manual of 1881.* Bottom: *Nesters at work, cutting the big boys down to size*

glaring flaw. Instead of reducing rustling, it fanned an ember into a blazing flame.

An even more heinous crime was the changing of a brand. It constituted the deliberate theft of marked property. This was accomplished by a 'running iron,' using a straight bar or, better yet, a heated wire. This did not deface the original brand, but rather added to it and thereby altered its entire appearance.

For example: *IO* became *7OI* ; or *7OL* became *ЯOB* ; ⊃—⊂, the wrench, could be altered to O—O, the bit, and so on. The rustler, like all thieves, had to be ingenious.

A certain basic antagonism existed between the growing number of small ranchers and the great established spreads, many of which were controlled by distant Eastern financial interests. It had long been accepted among the 'little fellas' that the big ranchers were too big, too rich and too powerful. Some cowboys blatantly made their living stealing cows and many small ranchers on the same basis justified helping themselves by boldly cutting the barbed wire fences and driving the cattle home.

The big ranches really were too vast for their cowboys to guard their lines effectively. And the little ranchers—the rustlers—gloated at the idea of bringing the 'big boys' to their knees. Many times small ranchers were helped by the very cowboys employed by the Eastern interests, who in sympathizing with the economic struggle of the little fellas, would themselves be a 'little on the rustle.' As a matter of fact, so determined were a great number of cowboys and small ranchers to destroy and ruin the huge ranches financed by absentee owners, that rustling became a way of life.

So strong was the feeling against the absentee owners that a cowboy loyal to his employer was sneeringly referred to as a 'pliers man' on the basis that he had to spend so much time mending the wire fences which the rustlers cut.

All this is not to say that the big boys didn't fight back. Between the years 1876 and 1886 dozens of Montana rustlers were either lynched or shot by vigilantes. Thirteen men were found strung up on a railroad bridge on one day alone. Many more were brought to trial. Bringing a rustler to justice, however, was a far cry from obtaining a conviction. In northern Wyoming, the home base of the rustlers, the jury and the judge were local residents. The judge himself had been elected by the very men who were doing the rustling; the jury was composed entirely of active cattle thieves. Acquittal was almost a foregone conclusion.

By 1892 the situation reached such a critical point that the cattle kings gathered in Cheyenne, Wyoming to take positive action. By now their change purses were shrunken to the size of a dead mouse skin from the loss of cattle. Their plan was to hire professional gunmen and proceed to clean out the rustlers in their Johnson County lair. And so, on April 7, 1892, a little army, calling themselves the 'Regulators Association,' composed of some forty cattle barons with their horses and gun-slingers, boarded a train bound from Cheyenne to Casper. There, in the early dawn, the men un-loaded their horses. Led by a Major Wolcott, they rode north toward Buffalo, the county seat and very core of all the trouble.

Near the Johnson County line, the column came upon the Kay Cee Ranch owned by Nathan Champion. Not only was he known to be a rustler, but worse still, an organizer of the 'Settlers' against the 'Regulators.' Lying in ambush, the invaders captured an old trapper who had left the cabin to get water. From him they learned that with Champion was his partner, Nick Ray, and another trapper, Ben Jones. Not long after, Ben Jones came down toward the barns, and like his friend walked straight into the barrels of the Winchesters. Wondering what had happened to the two trappers, Nick Ray stepped out the cabin door and was instantly downed—riddled in the head and body. Valiantly he dragged himself back to the cabin as Champion thrust open the door and fired, wound-ing one of the hired Texas gunmen. In spite of the barrage, Champion was able to drag his wounded friend inside. Here, barricaded, Champion held off his assailants from early morning till about three o'clock that afternoon. In the meantime, his partner had died, but Champion had wounded two more of his attackers.

At mid-afternoon a settler named Black Jack Flagg approached the Champion ranch. He was riding a horse, accompanied by his nephew driving a buckboard. As they drew near, they discovered the siege. Unharnessing the horse from the wagon and escaping the Regulators' fierce bullets, they galloped north to warn their friends and neighbors.

The cattle barons and their hired guns decided they must act quickly if they were to win their battle with the heroic Champion. Bravely they captured Mr. Flagg's abandoned buckboard, and piling it with sticks and hay, set fire to it and pushed it against the cabin. It didn't take long for the flames to consume the side of the log house. Choked by smoke, Champion burst from his burning home,

shooting as he came, only to die in a blaze of fire from a host of Winchesters.

Unbelievably, Champion kept a running diary throughout the entire siege. His last entry was, 'The house is all fired. Goodbye boys, if I never see you again.'

The Regulators left the Kay Cee Ranch, left the burning cabin, left the body of Champion with a big note stuck on his chest: CATTLE THIEVES BEWARE.

The ridiculous army then continued north. They had the names of some seventy rustlers to whom they intended to teach a little lesson. About fourteen miles south of Buffalo, at the T A Ranch, they were met by their forward scout, Phil Defrau. He re-ported that a hundred or so angry and determined men were riding hard in their direction. The rifles and sidearms they brandished looked like proof of their intentions.

Mr. Flagg had been entirely successful in warn-ing the settlers. Red Angus, the sheriff of Buffalo must have pretty well exhausted his supply of tin badges in deputizing volunteers. Recruits swarmed in, it was their necks or else.

Now the tables were turned. In the shadows of the Big Horn Mountains, the Regulators, out-numbered two to one, frantically began to dig fortifications to barricade the T A Ranch. Here the hunters had become the hunted. Barely had they got themselves readied when riders appeared along the horizon. Some shots were fired and returned. The siege had begun. The Johnson County men moved in, pushing bales of hay before them as shields. Meanwhile, as more and more recruits arrived, the settlers rigged up a moveable contrap-tion to which they set fire, a sort of flaming smoke-screen. The cattle barons were going to enjoy a little bit of their own medicine, about three days of it.

And then, just as the defenders were adjusting to the idea of being roasted, the blatant sound of a bugle was heard in the distance. In no time, not one, not two, but three troops of United States Cavalry appeared, took matters in hand, stopped the fight-ing and spoiled all the fun. The comic three-day Johnson County War ended before it got started.

Two men, each greedy, unscrupulous and willful, were the cause of New Mexico's infamous Lincoln County War. John Chisum and Major L. G. Murphy were destined to be antagonists. The record suggests Chisum smelled somewhat less putrid than Murphy.

John Chisum, a Texan with considerable success as a trail driver, tried his hand at the meat-packing business, only to run up debts amounting to as much as $90,000. Unable to pay, he mockingly turned his back on his creditors, drove a herd of Longhorns west, and made a masterful plan.

He decided ranching might be his forte and the Pecos territory of New Mexico might be his country. He was correct on both counts. Over the years he built up his herd until he had 100,000 cattle; and he acquired land as well, much of it as a squatter, until his holdings were the size of the state of Pennsylvania.

So vast was his ranch, so numerous were his Longhorns, that his cowboys were hard pushed to patrol them. The rustlers were aware of this and reveled in the easy pickings. Despite his famous brand—the 'long rail' which stretched from shoulder to flank—and a split ear mark which gave a cow the appearance of having four ears and gave his ranch the nickname 'Jingle Bob,' Chisum, the King of the Pecos, was robbed blind. As if to add insult to injury, when he was able to catch some thief red-handed, the culprit invariably escaped the Lincoln County jail with the greatest of ease.

Major L. G. Murphy, formerly from California, settled in Lincoln where he owned the general store, the saloon, a ranch and the sheriff. Because his cattle herd was not extensive, people wondered how he managed to market so many steers each year. John Chisum didn't wonder. Angered at his losses, he flatly accused Murphy of rustling his cattle. Murphy sneered at the insult, but he did employ young Alexander McSween, an attorney, to represent him.

J. H. Tunstall was a very rich Englishman lured to the West by its rugged romance. Near Lincoln he bought himself a ranch. His attire, like his speech, was very British and at first he was an

object of ridicule to the rough cowboys. But he was straightforward and affable, so much so that he soon won the respect not only of his men, but of neighboring ranchers. Tunstall was no weak cup of tea. Among his cowhands was an unprepossessing but likable boy of five foot seven inches named William Bonny.

John Chisum was still losing cattle and the rustlers were still escaping from jail. And then one day the Jingle Bob cowhands caught some Murphy men red-handed with such incontrovertible evidence that the Murphy cowboys were held for trial. Murphy ordered Mr. McSween to defend his men, but to everyone's amazement and Murphy's ire, the young lawyer flatly refused. The rustlers were so blatantly guilty that McSween's ethics overruled his legal training. Murphy was infuriated, but helpless.

Shortly afterwards, John Chisum decided to retain McSween to represent his legal interests. As if fate were offering a further insult to Major Murphy, the pleasant Englishman opened a general store in Lincoln in direct opposition to Murphy's monopoly. And he hired McSween to manage the business. When the Tunstall operation began to succeed, putting a crimp in Murphy's business, John Chisum, with Tunstall's money, opened a bank at the rear of the building and became its president.

To add fuel to the feud, McSween thwarted Murphy in an inheritance case in deference to the heir. Murphy retaliated by charging McSween with embezzlement, whereupon the young attorney transferred his property to Tunstall.

This was too much for Murphy. He sent a deputized posse to Tunstall's ranch with orders to retrieve in cattle what he thought was due to him in the inheritance and to bring Tunstall in too. After considerable argument, Tunstall agreed and fearlessly rode to town with the posse, accompanied by his ranch-hands. These included William Bonny, who rode ahead. Suddenly, without any reason (except perhaps the drunkenness of the posse members) shots rang out. Horrified, Bonny watched as his boss, benefactor and friend fell dead. But he kept his head well enough to make a mental note of every posse member responsible for the crime. Little did Murphy or his men realize that William Bonny was the outlaw, Billy the Kid, who had killed his first man at the age of twelve and was one of the West's most courageous, deadly and ruthless gunmen.

Chisum and McSween were fortunate to have Billy the Kid and his gunmen on their side, but Murphy balanced matters out by hiring gun-slingers of his own.

The stage was now set for a pretty good war. As the months passed, little armies of cowboys ambushed one another, sheriffs were shot down, ranch-hands bushwhacked.

In a pitched battle in Lincoln, the Murphy men cornered McSween and his followers in his own house and then set fire to it. As the heat and smoke intensified, McSween's wife and some female friends were forced to leave. As they walked out of the door, not a shot was fired. But as for the men, when they ran out, each was met with a hail of bullets, including McSween himself. Soon the choking smoke became unbearable and the remaining men burst out. Scurrying in bunches, racing hither and yon, they made a miraculous escape. Billy the Kid was the last to leave. As he blazed his way to freedom he killed one man and wounded two others.

With McSween gone, the war took on the spirit of a vendetta. The Kid began evening the score until nearly every man responsible for Tunstall's death was dead or about to become a corpse. Pat Garret, the relentless sheriff of Lincoln County, who had doggedly tracked the Kid for months, finally surprised him in a friend's house on the night of July 14, 1881, and shot him dead. Only twenty-one years old, Billy the Kid is said to have killed twenty-one men (not counting Mexicans and Indians) in his short career of assassination.

With his death, the Lincoln County War came to a close. Murphy, destitute from the drain of money paid to his killers, died before the Kid was killed. Chisum quit the whole business and they buried him in Arkansas three years later.

Nature had its way of making life difficult for the cattleman; in fact thunderstorms, droughts and blizzards could spell ruin. The worst example of nature's wrath began on the last day of December, 1885. The autumn had been a gentle one with an Indian Summer that went on and on, until the afternoon of December 31. Then, from the north came a mild drizzle, slowly the temperature fell, quietly soft white flakes drifted in the air. And thus commenced the greatest blizzard the cattlemen had ever seen. For three days the white death surged in from the north, driving before it all the cattle in its path. From the Dakotas to Texas the cattle drifted, halted only by the drift fences or in cuts and coulees beyond which they could not pass.

Many cowboys, aware of the imminent tragedy, rode after their herds in what proved a hopeless failure at rescue. Too often they themselves froze, and like their cattle, were later found near their dead ponies in the shelter of some gulch.

The blizzard of '86 was disaster. Cattle carcasses by the tens of thousands were found, often hundreds of miles from their home ranches. Losses were astronomical. The OS Ranch in Kansas lost nearly 11,000 head, while the Circle M's losses were over 5,000. Considering similar deaths in the Dakotas, Nebraska, parts of Arizona and Colorado, this destruction was appalling.

The next summer was cursed by drought. The cattle that survived the blizzard found pickings sparse. By fall, the cows were walking rib cages with taut-stretched hides. Winter came early this year. The first snow fell in October. While there were no raging blizzards, the snows fell and fell and covered the grasslands so the cattle couldn't graze. Horses will paw through the snow to reach the grass, while cows go to the low country where the grass grows tallest. However, if the grass is deeply covered, cattle just stand there with their backs humped up and starve to death. The heavy storms of the winter of '86 were west of those of the previous year, so what cattle were spared the previous year were now destroyed. When spring came, the stockmen counted up their losses and a great many just quit. Among them were the Swan

64

Above: Cowboy Camp During the Roundup *by Charles M. Russell*. Below: Roping a Maverick *by Charlie Dye*. Above right: A Tight Dally and a Loose Latigo *also by Russell*. Below right: Bronc in a Cow Camp *by Russell*

Land and Cattle Company which lost 5,400 steers and folded, while the Worsham Cattle Company didn't even bother to reckon the ruin.

No one activity was more critical to the cattlemen than the roundup. It was thought of as the culmination of a year's work, but in reality it was the payoff of a daring gamble. It was the time to take inventory and to count the harvest. If the calf crop was high and the market was up, it was good times for the rancher. Conversely, if poor conception, rustlers, blizzards or drought had taken their toll, the stockman could be hurt and hurt badly.

In the 1880s and 1890s, the roundup usually took place in midsummer. Very often neighboring ranchers joined forces. Despite the efforts of the line riders, cattle from one ranch invariably mixed with cattle of another and now was the time to 'throw them over' to the land of the proper owner. A 'captain' was chosen to supervise the roundup and he in turn selected a 'lieutenant,' each with a group of cowboys. In general the lieutenants were the foremen of the co-operating ranches, for they knew best their own territory and their own men.

Originally, corrals were set up at a centrally

XIT

Cortez's Three Crosses

Walking A

Flying W

Rocking Chair

Lazy K

V Bar Backward L

Four Sixes

Heart over Heart

Cow

J connected F over Mill Iron

Dinner Bell

2 connected 4

Tumbling 3

Diamond Bar

Quarter Circle, Upside Down Y,
Quarter Circle

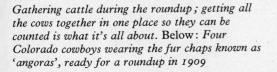

convenient point where the cattle would be gathered, but since these were often at an isolated spot, rustlers discovered that they made a most advantageous place to carry out their nefarious operations. The big ranchers learned quickly, tore the corrals down and used one or another's home ranch for sorting, counting, branding and steering.

The area of a roundup might involve as much as 4,000 square miles. Within the boundaries might be between 5,000 and 10,000 cows, scattered here and there in little bunches, hidden in watered draws, spread out on the 'flats,' secluded in the shade of the ponderosa pines. It was the cowboy's job to bring them in—to sweep the range clean.

Gathering the cattle was no easy task. The cowboys were sent out to the far reaches of the range. At first a man might find four or five head, then possibly another ten or twelve. These he would drive toward the main corrals. Owing to the natural tendency for cattle to herd, the bunches grew larger and larger. A cowboy driving one bunch would meet another and the two herds would combine. At length three or four men might be driving as many as 100–300 animals. When finally all the cows were assembled, which could take several days, the real work began—that of 'cutting out' and branding.

From among the cowmen was chosen a 'tally-

The day's work of a cowpuncher, even today,
alternates moments of tranquility (left) with
sequences of the hard-driving action portrayed by
Charles Russell in Jerked Down (below) and
W. A. Rodgers in Cutting Out (below left)

Left: *Heeling : this roped critter will now be dragged to the men branding near the gate.*
Below left: *Branding irons : the smaller irons were used for calves since the mark grows with the calf.*
Right: *The rope : the essential 'long arm' of the cowboy*

man,' someone of reliable character who would keep count of what cattle belonged to each owner. Cattle were 'cut out' or sorted for several purposes, first to brand the unmarked calves, then to 'beef cut' or ascertain the cowman's harvest so as to select the fat animals for market.

Cutting out the calves for branding took skill, a quick eye and, the prize of every cowboy—the cutting horse. Almost by instinct, these little cow ponies seemed to realize which cow and calf were to be separated from the herd. A good cowboy can indicate with the slightest motion of his body, the barest push of his knee, the gentlest touch of the rein, just which cow he wants separated and, as if by magic, the pony gets the message. He goes at his task with an uncanny spirit of enthusiastic loyalty. There is no more marvelous sensation than to be working on a good cutting horse—man and beast silently communicating to make the perfect team.

In separating a cow and its calf from the herd, the instinct of the calf to hang close to its mother no matter where she went, was of great help in determining ownership. When the pair was separated, the calf was branded with the mother's mark, and the little fellow was added to the tally of the cow's owner.

As the pair was cut out, the calf was roped. Sometimes the cowboy would loop his lariat over the doggie's neck, often he would 'heel rope' it and then drag the bawling critter toward the branding irons.

The irons were heated in a long fire pit, heated till they were scarlet red. Irons for each ranch were readied and the tally-man totaled the branded calves belonging to each stockman. As the calf was dragged to the fire, two men grabbed him, one at the head, the other by the tail. Holding the calf down by stretching it out, the brander could plant his iron hard on the sizzling flank of the struggling calf. With that stroke, the little animal became the legal property of the J Bar C Outfit.

If the men were holding down a bull calf, it was customary for one man, equipped with a sharp knife, to 'steer' him. In one painful instant, such a calf was destined to become one of a future year's

Roping a maverick may go smoothly or it may turn into the sort of incident cowboys have bad dreams about, like Russell's Broken Rope. Below right: Meals at a roundup were just short of elegant, generally consisting of the basic beans, bacon and coffee

crop of beef. With the job done, the little steer was released to scamper off in search of its mother.

When the day's work was finished, the cowboys gathered around their respective camps—each ranch having set up its own chuck wagon and remuda. Here it was that 'cookie' set out his repast. He might serve up a concoction of kidney stew, affectionately referred to as 'son-of-a-gun stew;' or maybe 'county attorney,' a stew made of veal, this complemented by canned corn, soda sinkers and black coffee so strong a spoon was sure to float.

After nightfall, those cowboys not assigned to sing to the cattle might exchange tall tales or sing among themselves. With the cows safely corralled, a cowhand might even break out a banjo.

After the calves were branded and steered, the

'beef cut' took place. It was now that cattle, especially the fat ones, were separated from the herd and held in readiness to be driven to the nearest railhead. The tally-man was busy keeping records of precisely how many beeves properly belonged to each ranch.

And so the roundup ended. Men were assigned to drive the beeves to the railhead and here the tally was finally recorded. Each owner was now credited and often paid for what was due him. More often than not there were buyers right at the corrals, but sometimes the ranchers waited for the money until the livestock, crowded in the drafty cattle cars, finally reached Kansas City or Chicago.

It was at roundup time, with so many cowboys gathered together, that the customs of these tough men might best be observed. Never was there such a collection of bowlegged characters gathered at one spot—their knees bent from years in the saddle. A cowboy was a very awkward man when on foot. Walking was not only unnatural, it was immoral. The only sensible, the only human form of locomotion was astride a horse. And while the bent-legged, hunchbacked cowboy could barely navigate on foot, on a horse he was transformed into a gallant, dashing hero.

The cow pony is a remarkable animal. As Texans introduced 'hot-blooded' stallions from the East, the Thoroughbred, the Quarter Horse and the Morgan (which itself was very likely a Quarter Horse), the wild mustang was upgraded. The Quarter Horse was bred at first as a racehorse which with a quick start could run the quarter mile in record time. As inheritor of the endurance, sure-footedness and toughness of the mustang, coupled with the speed and good disposition of the Quarter Horse, the cow pony is indispensable to the cowboy.

In general, the cow pony is close-coupled, enabling him to turn very sharply. He tends not to be a large horse, rarely standing over fifteen hands high. Cow ponies come in a variety of colors from bays to blacks, from roans called 'buckskins' to piebalds more commonly referred to as 'pintos' or 'paints.' Some, like the Palaminos, which are golden-colored horses, and the Appaloosa, which sports spots and blotches, especially around the rump, are considered now to be separate breeds.

Breaking a horse is a difficult task requiring patience, skill and courage. An untamed colt is wild and nervous. There are many techniques used for breaking a raw horse and some cowboys become specialists. One method is to wait until the horse is about four years old—by then it will have

matured enough to have some horse-sense. First he must be petted and haltered and led around the corral. Next the cowboy shows him a blanket and then a saddle, all the time patting and smoothing the frightened colt from nose to hocks. A good idea is to wave a gunnysack around its face and between its legs to get the animal used to fluttering objects so that later it won't shy. It's also especially important to acquaint him with a yellow oilskin slicker. A horse unfamiliar with this type of raincoat will most likely buck and heave, to the misfortune of everyone nearby, while a 'slickered' horse is a pleasure to ride.

The colt is then gently, carefully saddled and allowed to spend the day walking around the corral to get accustomed to the feel of the weight. Finally, the cowboy gingerly mounts the horse, riding it around the ring, hoping not to get bucked off. Such an animal which has never worked cows, never really been tested, is known as 'green broke.' This method of breaking a horse may take several days.

Not all cowboys have the time or patience to break a horse in this fashion. Some men just rope them, hobble them, saddle them, climb aboard and 'let 'er buck.' Such a 'bronco buster' literally wears down the horse and 'breaks' him. This is a quick and effective method, provided the horse is not so

Our $2.65 Pommel Yellow Slicker or Saddle Coat.

This coat is gotten up especially for horseback riders; made from yellow slicker, very heavy cloth, and makes the most perfect rain coat ever manufactured for the use of the horseman. This coat covers the entire saddle, as well as rider, thus insuring a dry seat, while the lower part is wide enough to cover the length of the rider. It is a combination coat, which can be made from a riding to a walking coat by simply adjusting one of the buttons. The best coat obtainable; has patent eyelet fasteners, non-corrosive zinc buttons; all of the latest improvements. Guaranteed to be strictly waterproof, and the best coat of its kind ever put on the market. Sizes, 36 to 44 inches breast measure; cut full and large.
No. 27R118 Price, each.....................$2.65

Above left: *Branding, cutting and inoculating. This calf's misery will end in less than a minute.* Top: *Breaking a horse is a job for the specialist.* Above: *The 'Slicker' or Saddle Coat which covered both rider and saddle*

Frederic Remington

Our Olympia Heavy High Grade Cowboy Saddle.

$31.85

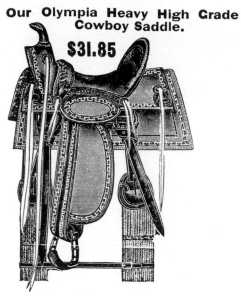

No.10R8015

spirited as to be unbreakable. And some horses are.

A cow pony is quick, alert, willing, gentle and somehow, almost instinctively, knows how to cope with cattle. If he doesn't have these qualities, he isn't much use. A good horse, like a good friend, is dependable.

As one old cowpoke said to another as they turned their horses out in the night pasture after ten hours in the saddle, 'You know, by God, Walt, I love that damn horse so much I like him.'

A cowhand might or might not own a horse, but he surely owned a saddle. In a way it was his work bench and from it he did nearly all his chores. Like a well broken-in pair of boots, a saddle fitted a man. Since the cowboy spent from eight to ten hours a day astride it, it had to fit well. A man might lend his hat, his sixshooter, his chaps, even his horse, but his saddle never. A cowboy who had lost his shirt in gambling would rarely go so deep as to put up his saddle as a stake. The term 'he sold his saddle' was the equivalent of saying a man had 'sold his soul.'

The stock saddle is heavy, weighing from 40–50 pounds. It must be of such sturdy construction that the horn, with a rope looped or 'dallied' around it, can withstand the jerk and pull of a 2,000-pound bull. Its high cantle makes for easy, rocking chair-like riding, its heavy fenders protect the rider's legs. A wide latigo or girth, sometimes called *cincha*, ensures it staying secure on the horse. Equipped with leather strings, the cowboy could tie his lariat, bedroll and yellow slicker for ready use. There were many models, many styles, some plain, some elaborately tooled, but all good ones were built to withstand the toughest sort of strain. For the cowboy, his saddle was a most cherished possession. Everyone in the West knew it and as one cowpoke expressed it, 'There goes Buck with his $100 saddle on his $10 horse.'

While the saddle was obviously the cowboy's prime piece of equipment, his hat and chaps, his boots and spurs were pretty important too.

A cowboy's hat was a combination of parasol, to shade him from the sun, and umbrella, to protect him from the rains. Sometimes it was even used as a pail to quench a horse's thirst. In the South, black wide-brimmed hats were favored, while in Wyoming and Montana light-colored, narrow-brimmed hats were preferred. A wide-brimmed hat catches more wind and blows off more easily, yet a narrow brim isn't much for shade.

The cowboy boot, high-topped and high-heeled, with a pointed toe, was designed for a very real, very functional purpose. The high tops protected the cowboy's calf from chafing against the saddle's fender and from rattlesnake bites, should he have to dismount to tend to a sick calf. Most often the boots were stitched in a way to form fancy patterns, especially on and about the tops, just to pretty them up. The high heels not only kept his foot from slipping forward in the stirrup, but served as a brake, when, God forbid, he was roping cattle on foot. The pointed toe enabled the horseman to make easy the entry into the stirrup. Mounting a frisky horse was enough bother in itself. Fumbling around to get one's feet in the stirrups was more than bothersome, it was plain dangerous.

The spurs the cowmen wore were fashioned from the old Spanish styles, most often with vicious rowels. There were many modifications and some were fanciful, like the 'gal-leg' spur, the shank of which was modeled after a woman's leg. A good horseman used his spurs sparingly. Strangely, a good horse was made better by their mere presence.

The bridle and the bit, like the spur, were derived from Spanish patterns. The bit took many forms, each designed to control the horse. Some bits, like the spade and the ring, were veritably lethal and some curb bits could be pretty authoritative. The idea of a harsh bit was to stop a headstrong horse, for all too often the half-tamed mustang or wild bronco was willful to the point of defiance.

The proficiency of a cowboy depended in large measure upon his ability to 'rope.' Throwing a rope required much practice and some men achieved a masterful skill.

The lariat was, in reality, a flying noose. Some thirty to sixty feet in length, the rope was threaded through itself between a smaller loop or hondo, to make a big loop. Thrown by the skillful cowboy it could capture the most wayward cow or mustang.

With all his equipment, rope and saddle, spurs and hat and horse, it took more than that to make a cowboy. It took practiced skill and cold courage. As one man described him, 'A cowboy is a man with guts and a horse.'

Stockmen and Cowboys on the Modern Ranch

The cowboy on the modern ranch is nothing more than a chip off the old block. He still wears the wide-brimmed hat, the high-heeled boots, and he still tends the cows. But techniques, differing marketing procedures, improved breeds and changing economic conditions have altered the cowboy's way of life. Strangely, it's been a change in degree only, not at all in kind. And this is simply because a cow is a cow.

The cattle have changed too. Replacing the Texas Longhorns were English breeds, cattle that were more efficient, cattle that were compact, cattle that were economically better suited to the times.

The Durham, now called the Shorthorn, had been popular in the East, particularly because of its good beef quality combined with the propensity for producing large amounts of milk.

The men at the King Ranch of Texas, owners of the largest spread in the United States, were in 1910 given an unusual gift—a tremendous bull which was half Brahman and half Shorthorn. Impressed by the size and adaptability of this East Indian cross to intense heat and little water, the King ranchers crossed Shorthorn cows with the offspring of this gift bull, whom they called Monkey. They named this cross Santa Gertrudis and to this day these cattle are recognized as producers of very large calves peculiarly adjusted to the hot southern climate.

The most popular, and in many ways the most thrifty breed, however, was the Hereford, familiarly referred to as the 'whiteface.' These hardy animals so dominated the range country that in essence they became *the* beef cow of the West.

The Aberdeen Angus, long popular among eastern stockmen for their high cutability—that percentage of usable meat to total carcass weight—only lately found favor with western cattlemen. In recent years they have been in growing demand.

Not only do they calve more easily, which means a higher percentage calf crop, but their black skin makes them less susceptible to eye cancer and sunburned teats and udders—an ailment sometimes caused by the reflection of the sun against the snow, which is so painful to the mother cow she will not permit her calf to nurse. These factors, combined with the quality of the beef, make the Angus readily marketable.

Ed C. Lasater, a farseeing Texas and Colorado stockman, crossed some Brahman bulls with his Hereford and Shorthorn herds. After a rigid culling program, which included such factors as disposition, weight and confirmation, Lasater was so pleased with the results he named his new breed 'Beefmaster.'

In 1936, the men at the King Ranch bought two huge, white bulls from one Jean Pugibet, a French stockman, operating a hacienda in Mexico. Pugibet had made a visit to France and was much impressed by this great breed called Charolais. In recent years, their popularity has increased, due in large measure to their great size (bulls weighing from 2,000–2,500 pounds) and the high amount of lean meat in proportion to excess fat.

Most recently, certain so-called 'exotic' breeds are being introduced to American ranches. Without exception they are continental cattle of immense size. From France come the Simmental and Limousin, from Italy the Chianina and from Germany the Gelbvich. They are beefy and they are chunky and so long in the loin you can count the extra steaks in any one of them just by 'eyeballing' them. For the stockman, that's where the real money is, in those tenderloins and sirloins. Each claim certain advantages such as good cutability, low fat weight in proportion to red meat, high rate of gain in calves. These are factors of grave importance to the stockman whose chief aim, if he is to stay in business, is to sell the most 'steaks'

The white bulls of the French Charolais breed often tower six feet above the ground

Left, top to bottom: *Three breeds of beef cattle: Black Angus, Limousin and Hereford. A stockman needs at least one bull for 20 cows.* Above: *Shorthorns, first of the English breeds introduced to the West and still popular among some cattlemen*

for the lowest cost of production. How good they will prove to be depends, among other things, upon how well they adapt to the particular environmental conditions of the ranches. At the moment, they are being toted partly because of their bull's ability to impart hybrid vigor to their offspring. Cows of the recognized English breeds, impregnated with sperm of the exotics, produce calves possessing exceptional size.

Geneticists have long been aware of the principle of hybrid vigor and stockmen have put the principle to practical use. By crossing, for example, Charolais bulls with Angus cows, ranchers have found that the offspring gain weight much more rapidly and achieve greater size in much less time. This particular cross produces steaks with more red meat, less fat and good marbling. Marbling is that thin lining of fat appearing within the red meat which gives a steak a special flavor that an all-red

piece of meat does not possess. Since the stockman sells his beef on the hoof for so many cents a pound, the heavier the calf, the more money per unit he can expect to receive. And since the buyers, beginning with the feeders, next the slaughter-house, then the retail butcher and finally the housewife pay more for tasty, tender beef, an animal which possesses in his makeup both a great number of steaks as well as chop-licking ones is the stockman's dream come true.

The mere size of these European cattle is start-ling. There is a marvelous story of the Colorado rancher who, in this case, bought himself twenty head of Charolais bulls, hopefully to begin a profitable cross-breeding program. The bulls arrived a little after dark, a little past schedule, a little later than midnight. This, the rancher figured, was about par for the course. Cattle truckers, for some unknown reason, set their clocks differently

from other people. The bulls were big and ranted around so violently in the corrals that the rancher decided to turn them loose in his 300-acre east pasture rather than have them tear down his pens. He knew right then and there he'd bought himself a ranch full of big action.

Bright and early the next morning, the Colorado stockman mounted his dependable cow pony, as experienced a buckskin quarter horse as you could ever set your saddle on, to check out his new high-priced purchase. He rode toward a ridge behind which he hoped to find the bulls. Suddenly, as the horseman reached the summit, several five- to six-foot-high white beasts stood strong against the horizon. So big, so huge, so unbelievably impressive were they that the stockman's horse stopped dead in her tracks and trembled. It's one thing for a man to be impressed by cattle, but it's another thing for a seasoned cow horse to be stunned.

The upgrading of American cattle has been accomplished over a long period of time by mating average or 'grade' cows with 'pure-blooded' or 'registered' bulls. During the last quarter of the nineteenth century, a majority of cattle herds were composed of pretty nondescript animals, but as the buyers shifted from purchasing by the 'head' to buying by the 'pound,' quality began to assume an economic importance. Now the aim of the stockman was to produce animals with good weight and tastier beef.

To achieve this, the cattle ranchers, the men who ran the great herds of commercial cows or so-called grade animals, saw the advantage of putting registered bulls with their cows. The breeders of pedigreed Shorthorn bulls such as the Bates Duchess line, promoted their stock as possessors of such potency that their offspring fell heir to the same high-quality characteristics the sires themselves possessed.

On the basis of this theory, ranchers over the years have purchased high-quality bulls of various breeds to improve the standard of their calf crop and in turn increase the price the stockman receives for his product. It is these very stockmen who work to produce the kind of beef which the consumers demand, all the beef eventually purchased by the housewife. These are the men who raise grade cattle, the great commercial herds which constitute the backbone of the American cattle industry.

The men who specialize in pure-bred cattle, the registered Hereford or Charolais, Angus or Santa Gertrudis, are breeders in perfection. To be successful they must become superbly knowledgeable and accomplished in all aspects of animal husbandry. They are a combination of geneticists and showmen, animal lovers and salesmen, herdsmen and accountants.

They may operate a large spread or a small, entirely specialized farm. They carry out their programs not only in every state in the Union, but in Canada and Mexico as well.

The herds of pedigreed cattle may number from twenty-five to fifty head to several hundred. Sires are advertised with emphasis not only upon their confirmation, but upon records of the proficiency of their progeny to gain weight rapidly and possess a carcass of high quality. Other features which the breeders claim for their stock include statements that their bulls will settle more cows in a minimum of time, will cover more country and not 'hang around the water hole.'

The breeders go to considerable effort to present their stock to the 'cow and calf' men, those ranchers who purchase registered bulls either to upgrade or maintain the quality of their so-called commercial herds. A good bull not only can produce fine calves which in turn bring more money at the market, but the quality of the herd itself can be improved by keeping the first-class heifers. By making them part of the herd while culling cows of inferior caliber, a rancher can improve his entire stock to meet the changing demands of the market place.

The competition to sell the registered animal is intense. Full-page ads in color in such magazines as the *Western Livestock Journal* boast of the desirability not only of one breed over another, but of one strain against another. Handsome pictures show massive bulls, docile cows and alert calves. Even colored shots of a carcass showing a mouth-

Left: *Scenes at a cattle show. The judges generally stand to the bull's left, checking the loins with their right hands. Below left: The ten animals judged best of their breed, posing for the crowd. Below: A Grand Champion from Texas*

watering, luscious rib eye steak are presented to lure the stockmen into making a purchase.

Advertising takes another tack in the cattle business, that of the great cattle shows. These exhibitions, held in the large cities of the West, give the breeder the chance to show his cattle in competition with the animals of other stockmen, as well as to sell them. The cattle are greatly pampered, washed and brushed and curried to the point of loving perfection. Sometimes they are given a bottle of beer just before show time to fill them out and give them a 'bloom.' Ladies' hair spray is especially effective in giving the coat a lustrous sheen.

Judges, most often college professors who teach animal husbandry, award prizes both in money and ribbons. To the exhibitor, the color of the ribbon is as important as the hardness of the cash.

For a stockman, especially when he is exhibiting registered bulls, the award of a blue ribbon as first prize or a purple one to mark a champion is as valuable an achievement as the performance record of the bulls themselves. The reason for this is that owning a prizewinner is the kind of promotion a stockman dreams of. It puts his cattle on the map.

In principle, the owner of such a champion does not sell his prize animal, but rather keeps it for breeding purposes and promotional advantage. More often, it is the offspring of these champions that are sold to the cow-calf stockmen.

When, however, the prizewinners are offered for sale, either on the auction block or by 'private treaty' they often bring excessively high prices. Today, the figure of $100,000 for a prize bull is by no means unheard of. The purchaser of these high-priced animals is rarely the cow-calf operator. Rather it is the stockman running registered cows who makes such outlays to improve his herd.

There's a standing joke among the men who run commercial herds and it is directed precisely at the high prices quoted in the newspapers about the sale of prize bulls.

'Yeah,' said Slim, as he looked at the latest quotation of $103,000 for a pedigree Hereford. 'I believe it sure helps to keep the values up.'

'How's that?' questioned Tex.

'Well, it makes a fella think they must have pretty high-toned stuff.'

'Right, but I never paid over $500 for a bull and I'm still in business.'

'Tell you what let's do,' barked Slim. 'I'll just buy that gimpy six-year-old whiteface bull of yours for $75,000 and send a notice to the *Daily Times*. We'll get a picture of you holding the check and me holding the bull.'

'And then,' croaked Tex, 'I'll buy that stove-in four-year-old Angus sire of yours for $75,000 and we'll do the same thing. It's a sure way to pleasure and profit in the cattle business.'

The point is, many of the registered beasts are overrated and overpriced, for understandable reasons. The owner, and in some cases, the owners —a group of speculators—have considerable money invested in a bull. Owners must promote the animal to the fullest extent if they are to receive a respectable return on their dollar.

The desire, the ambition of stockmen to possess top animals very often reaches the level of absurdity. There is the amazing case of some investors who purchased a prizewinning Angus bull for around $50,000, only to discover the beast was impotent. These naive speculators didn't have wit enough to have the bull's fertility tested. Nor did they have any recourse, for in the cattle business, unless otherwise specified, the rule is 'buy as is.'

Cattle exhibitions give the cow-calf man an opportunity to see, all gathered in one place, bulls— single bulls, pens of three and five, bulls of varied breeds and prices. From these he may select suitable sires for his herd. Many sales are made at these shows and, in general, ranchers obtain fine bulls from honest stockmen.

However, the stock shows in which prize animals compete for championships are in large measure for the benefit of the breeders of registered stock. Prizewinning steers attest to the quality of the breeder's line. Fashionable hotels, elegant restaurants and supermarket chains buy the fat animals for promotional purposes, thus placing their establishments before the public as purveyors of fine beef. While the rancher may expect to receive at auction thirty or even forty cents a pound, the Grand Champion steer may bring many dollars a pound on the auction block. This wide gap in prices can make a cow-calf operator cry.

A case in point, one which is enough to raise the temper of every commercial cowman in the country, was the story of a 1971 Grand Champion, 'Big Mac.' This handsome Black Angus was bought at auction by McDonald's Hamburgers, a huge chain of drive-in restaurants, for eleven dollars and forty cents per pound. Later, however, it was discovered that 'Big Mac' was losing his beautiful black color and, strange to say, was turning white. Closer examination proved that the champion was not an Angus at all, but in reality a handsome, creamy colored Charolais steer which had been dyed. The sale was voided, the judges embarrassed

and the owner's reputation jeopardized. For the student of the hoax, this was a wonderful one.

The average stockman, the cow-calf operator, pays from between $300–$1,000 for his herd sires. And he goes about buying those bulls in a variety of ways. He may either attend the important stock shows held in such cities as Denver, Fort Worth or Kansas City. He may read the ads in trade papers and go to a dispersal sale where a breeder of registered stock is selling off his crop of young bulls, or he may just climb in his pickup truck and visit ranches where he knows the stockman has a reputation for raising high-quality bulls.

Buying a bull is no easy matter. A surprising number of factors must be taken into consideration. It's quite exciting, even though it is all done in a very low key, to observe a first-class rancher bargain for the purchase of a topflight sire from a reputable breeder. The rancher looks at confirmation, length of the loins where the beef steaks are located, strength of legs. A reputable breeder will guarantee fertility through a veterinarian's test, at the time of shipment only.

Acquiring a good herd of cows demands just as much care as purchasing the bull. Established ranchers need to obtain cows to replace those they have culled for one reason or another, those that have died, strayed or been stolen. Sometimes a man makes a purchase to increase the size of his operation or to improve the quality of his herd. A new rancher, starting from scratch, has no choice but to buy cows.

Cattle are graded for their quality. Consideration is given to the carcass classifications from the highest 'prime' and 'choice' to the lowest 'canner' and 'cutter.' The stockman endeavors to acquire cows fitting the top quality. However, he is also interested in how easily she gives birth, her ability to give a good quantity of milk and her mothering instinct. It costs no more to keep a good cow than a poor one and her calves always bring a higher price on the market.

Most cattlemen go directly to the ranch to purchase cows. Here they can walk among the herd and 'fault' the animals, that is, point out the

negative characteristics of this cow or that. If the cattle pretty much come up to the standard of quality the buyer is considering, and the asking price, say $250 a head, is within the realm of the going market, then a shrewd cattle buyer will take the faults into account, using them as leverage when he offers to buy the cows at $200 each. In such transactions, called a 'private treaty,' cattle are bought and sold by the head, not by weight as calves are sold at the market.

Much dickering takes place when cattlemen buy and sell. Some crafty buyers even dress in worn and shabby clothes, giving the impression that they really can't afford to spend much. An alert seller, on the contrary, may wear the most stylish attire so that his well-groomed appearance will shed an aura of quality over his cattle. The buyer and seller may bargain for many minutes, or sometimes days, making counter-offers until one or the other gives in and they make a deal and shake hands.

Buying cattle is only one of the many activities of ranchers. Some of the work is seasonal, like making hay, other chores such as feeding the bulls and horses are daily ones. Life on a working ranch changes with the seasons.

Winter is a time of feeding the herd and of repairing machinery. In the northern Plains just getting the equipment operable in weather thirty to forty below zero can be a half-day's job.

The ranch-hand atop a wobbling hay wagon (known as a 'hay rack,') who dumps off hay bales weighing from 80–85 pounds to the hungry cows, which follow along like strings of boys chasing an ice-cream vendor, may or may not fully appreciate his role in the economics of the cattle business. If the wind is up to 30 miles an hour, the temperature down to ten below zero and the icy snow blowing diagonally to hit him full in the face like tiny needles, he does know the general idea is to get the job done quickly. He also knows that if, for example, the herd numbers 600 head, he must load, and in turn dump off 150 bales of hay, for each cow needs a quarter of a bale, the equivalent of 20 pounds of grass per day. That is just about how many pounds of grass a cow consumes on summer pastures.

Mere hay is not enough if cows are to produce healthy calves. Feed must possess nutrients, particularly vitamin A, if the stockman's crop of

calves is going to approach the ideal 100 percent. Although properly harvested alfalfa possesses these standards, not all hay does. Thus commercial feeds, sometimes in pellet form, other times as loose and ground or rolled grains, are prepared to supplement what hay alone cannot provide.

Feeding cattle begins in early winter in the northern country—early because of the snows. The winter's cold freezes the streams, the ponds and the stock tanks nestled under the windmills—sometimes solid. In any case, a daily winter chore facing the cowboy is attacking the ice with axe and pitchfork to make a little waterhole. With the axe he chops the ice, with the pitchfork he removes the slabs so that the cows may drink. Chopping out a stream or stock pond is no major problem, except the cowboy can get plenty wet and plenty cold if the chips fly in his face or the ice breaks through. But cutting the ice in a stock tank requires caution. Woe to the careless cowboy who chops right through the tank only to lose gallons of precious water and gain the wrath of the foreman.

Spring, for a vast majority of ranches, is fence fixing time. If the rancher raises any crops, this is when he drills his oats or plants his corn. But most important, spring on a working ranch brings prospects of newborn calves, lettuce-green leaves on the cottonwoods, melting snow and mud.

There are various types of mud the cowboy contends with; red mud, cowpen mud—called 'crud'—and, worst of all, gumbo. Gumbo, light grayish in color, generally combines the slippery quality of vanilla ice-cream with the sticky character of bubble gum. Pickup trucks are especially susceptible to being mired, for if the driver doesn't slip off the road into the ditch, his tires can gather so much of the stuff in a matter of minutes that it binds in the fenders, enough to stall him to a dead stop. Ranching never was meant to be easy, but after shoveling snow, chopping ice, trying to start the machinery at twenty below zero—the cowboy can't get too het up over mud.

Spring is not all mud, for the cottonwoods do leaf out and in March and April the little calves arrive. When possible, climate permitting, the

rancher allows the cows to calve on the range. This arrangement is much more feasible in the southern Plains where the winters are less severe and the chances of the calves freezing to death are of no concern. On a well-managed northern ranch, however, the cowboys must bring the cows to the barns to calve. Customarily, the cowboy will ride among the herd carefully observing the 'heavy' cows, cows that will give birth within twelve hours or so. These are cut out of the herd and driven home at a slow gait to prevent harm both to the mother and her unborn offspring.

The cowboys watch the cows pretty intently, especially so-called 'first calf heifers.' These are young cows, very often no more than two years old, who are about to have their first calf. And not infrequently such new mothers need help. The good cowboy stays ready, ready to 'pull' a calf, if need be.

All sorts of trouble can develop at this time and the successful rancher must be pretty much his own veterinarian. 'Breech' presentations are not unheard of, while Caesarean operations are sometimes a necessary last resort. Possibly the greatest shock a cowboy receives is to be presented with a two-headed calf. These rarely live very long. The happy moment, however, is to hear the first tiny bawl of a normal baby, to watch its mother lick it clean as it teeters on its wobbly legs, trying to nurse, searching by instinct for that warm, life-giving milk. This just makes it worth staying up all night in a cold barn.

The cowman hopes for 100 percent calf crop, that is, that every cow he owns will bear a calf. This is not realistic unless a man owns one cow and it has one calf! But such a man is not a rancher. A cowman, however, can and should count on a 90–95 percent calf crop. Of this crop he must expect that about half will be bulls. These little critters will, by autumn, become his saleable crop, the chief source of his income. And it is in the late spring or early summer that the stockman readies his crop for sale.

The spring roundup is an exhilarating time. Now is when a rancher begins to speculate on his hopes for profits. Now he counts his calves which he equates with dollars. Now he hopes for a good fall calf market, counts on the summer rains bringing lush grass so the calves will fatten. This, of course, is just a hope. The eastern Colorado rancher, for example, knows full well that 13–15 inches of precipitation is the most he can expect for the entire year. It's a common saying among the stockmen of the arid West, as the sun rises bright and strong to the east, 'Well, Hank, we've got another goddam beautiful day.'

There is the sad yarn of the rancher who discovered a sick and bloated cow stuck in the mud at the edge of a stock pond. The cowboys roped the poor beast and dragged her out to the dried and crispy, withered grass. The men tried out everything they knew to revive the poor gal, but soon saw they were losing to the old man with the scythe. Tex was sent to call the 'vet' who, unbelievably, was available and arrived within an hour. Among other things, he recommended the cow be given an injection of glucose. Tex held the bottle of high-toned sugar water above his head to allow gravity to take effect and let the fluid run down the tube through the needle poked into the unfortunate cow. Everything worked well, so well, in fact, that the cow stood up and the cowboys cheered. And then the old cow stumbled, heaved an alarming sigh and dropped dead.

'What do you think killed her, Doc?' asked Tex.

'From the way she's bloated, I'd say lush grass.'

'Lush grass?' yelped Tex. 'We haven't had rain in ten weeks!'

Rounding-up means cutting out the calves to brand them. On some ranches it is done just as it was a century ago, but now more often the cows and calves are brought into corrals where the calves are separated. This the cowboys do by shooing out the cows, opening and closing gates, thus leaving the calves behind. Today rather than roping and throwing a calf to be branded, they are generally run through chutes into a 'squeeze.' This is a specially designed contraption composed of two parallel rows of bars which, when compressed, hold the animal firmly while it is being worked on.

97

Small squeezes, called 'calf cradles,' tip over so that the little animal lying prone can be treated more easily.

The cowboys literally push and prod the calves from a corral into the chutes and into the squeeze. Normally, five or six men are required, two to drive the calves, one to brand, one to inoculate against the calf-killing diseases, one to castrate the bull calves, referred to as 'steering,' and another to keep the irons hot. Ideally, a branding party also includes a couple of pretty women. They add to the morale and are a great help in opening the beer cans. A team such as this can work over 500 calves a day, about one calf per minute.

Many ranchers, particularly in the northern country, turn their bulls out shortly after branding time. The gestation period of a cow is 282 days, approximately nine months. Those cowmen wishing to have their cows calve, for example, in mid-March, turn the bulls out on or about 15 June. Ideally a rancher wants his calves born as early in the spring as possible so that his calf crop will have a long growing season to reach maximum weight

Below: *A cowhand may find the company of a good dog a real asset.* Bottom: *Cowgirls are rare but not unknown. Back in the 1880s the Becker* sisters of Alamosa, Colorado, *were hard at work branding cattle.* Right: *A Texas water-hole, mineral and salt blocks nearby*

for the fall market. Ranchers in the southern regions do not necessarily follow this system since they can calve all year round without fear of frozen animals.

Many cattlemen endeavor to have the calves born within a period of 30–45 days so that they will be of uniform size and weight at marketing time. Evenness is a highly desirable quality which buyers reward by paying a premium price.

To ensure high-quality calves and evenness, cattlemen are turning to artificial insemination. By spending from five to fifteen dollars, a stockman can often avail himself of the semen from a proven sire. Such an animal may be a champion worth $50,000. For the cowman, not only is artificial insemination a sound way to improve and upgrade his herd, but it has certain other advantages.

The stockman running six hundred head of cows expects to keep about thirty bulls, at a cost of possibly $750, making an investment of as much as $21,000. If, on the other hand, he pays ten dollars for an ampule of semen, he has an annual expense of $6,000. A range bull's effectiveness is not much more than five years, so the stockman can figure an annual cost of $4,200. But the stockman must feed his bulls all winter and take the chance of his animals becoming crippled (and thus useless), being infertile or falling sick and perhaps dying. These factors must be entered on the debit side of the ledger.

Artificial insemination, when properly carried out, offers the rancher a better chance to get all his

cows bred within the ideal period of 30–45 days. But this requires a knowledgeable and observant cowboy, one who can accurately detect when a cow is in heat. There are only twelve hours during which the sperm can fertilize the ovum. The cowboy, often the technician who performs the insemination, must be skillful. Failure at any step in this delicate business means a reduced calf crop. Realistic stockmen practicing AI rarely expect the high rate of conception that a well-operated ranch with range bulls can achieve. Therefore, many men using AI have a few 'follow-up' bulls as a kind of insurance to cover their mistakes.

In the summer the cowboy's time is divided between checking his calves, counting his cows and making hay. Hay is a prime crop, for it is the winter feed on a majority of American ranches.

Hay is cut and stacked in a variety of ways, partly due to regional differences, partly because of mechanized improvements. Essentially, haying involves mowing the grass or alfalfa at the proper time, allowing it to cure, and stacking it for winter storage. Hay used to be stored loose in haymows or great stacks. With the invention of the baling machine, it could be put up more quickly, stored more compactly and preserved more effectively. Other labor-saving devices like the swather, the accumulator and the automatic stacker have reduced the number of men required to make a ton of hay. It has not reduced the heat, the dust and much of the hard work. Making hay, at best, is about as glamorous as cleaning out a chicken house in mid-August.

Feed alone is not enough to make a cow thrive. Water is essential. Clear, running streams, referred to as 'live water,' are ideal, but cool water pumped by windmills, and stock ponds (small, man-made dammed-up lakes) are also valuable sources of supply. In summertime, troubles arise in periods of drought. Creeks run low, wells go dry, the water in stock ponds recedes. During such periods, the cowboys may have to carry water, often in old oildrums and tanks, to satisfy the animals. Even in good times, windmills must be oiled, pumps repaired.

Oiling the windmill is a tedious task. A cowboy may appear to be the epitome of confidence on a skittish horse, but atop the little windmill platform, 50–100 feet high, with the wind blowing, loosening bolts and pouring oil in a gearbox with one hand while holding on for dear life with the other is a scary job. It is really a bit beneath a cowboy's dignity.

In autumn, when the grass dries up and the yellow cottonwood leaves begin to drop, the fall roundup takes place. This is the culmination of a year's work, for now the rancher is gathering his harvest. This is the time of the auction sales where the calves are sold to the 'feeders.' These are the men who operate feed lots for the sole purpose of fattening calves to ready them for the slaughterhouse.

Steers and heifers are sold separately at market, steers bringing a slightly higher price. Therefore, the two sexes are often separated at this time. A stockman can generally expect his crop to be pretty equally divided between steers and heifers.

If the rancher plans to keep some of his heifers as replacements for his cow herd, now is the time the cowboys open and shut the corral gates culling the little females to determine which are best. Those heifers which meet a standard qualifying them to enter the herd are put in a special pen, later to be turned out with the cows, but only after they are completely weaned.

This is the time, too, that the range bulls are separated from the cows and placed either in especially strongly built bullpens or in a distant pasture to await reacquaintance with the cows the next spring.

The calves that are to be marketed are often weighed at this time. This not only gives the rancher an idea of what price his calves may bring, but more importantly, the rate of gain for each calf, which should be around three pounds a day.

For those ranchers who keep accurate records, this is vital information. A careful stockman gives a number to each cow, either by means of an ear tag (a number tag on a chain) or a number branded on her side. The latter is the best method, for it can never be lost. By checking his records with the calf's ear tag, attached at birth, the cowboy can determine the cow's performance as a mother. If her calf does not measure up, she will be sent to the butcher as a 'canner' or 'cutter,' to be replaced by a more efficient animal.

Sorting cattle in the fall is hard work. Either the corrals are filled with choking dust or they are a quagmire of mud and melting snow. To this is added the crescendo of bawling calves separated from their wailing mothers. The gates are heavy and must be opened and shut hundreds of times either to let a cow out or keep a calf in. Well-planned and sturdy corrals with adequate cutting pens and alleys make the job easier; poorly designed, rickety corrals are a nightmare. The cows and calves, of course, are anything but co-operative, and their desire to escape the pen and herd makes the job more exasperating. A cowboy on foot who is quick with the gate and a man on a good cutting horse are great assets. And it's also essential to have a ranchhand who can keep the records straight, who can count cattle accurately and read the brands and ear tag numbers without mistakes. Unless a stockman has cowboys who do this work well, the entire fall roundup can be an utter fiasco.

Just before the calves are ready for market, the ranchers must arrange for a brand inspection. In many western states the brands are registered and printed in a record book. An experienced inspector knows pretty well all the brands in his region. He, together with the stockman, walks among the calves to be sold confirming the marks and the tally. For a minimal fee per head, the rancher receives a certificate which in fact indicates to the buyer that he is not purchasing stolen cattle.

One problem that has plagued the cattleman from the beginning and has not been solved is rustling. Even with brand registrations and inspections—there are, for example, over 39,000 registered brands in Colorado alone—cowmen still lose many animals each year to thieves. The modern rustler now resorts to surveying a ranch in a small airplane to learn where the cattle may be grazing. Then, under cover of darkness, he and his cohorts,

Left: *One unhappy cow being treated to a mud bath. The mud is a special preparation for defeating parasites and other ills*

Above: *In Utah a group of steers await brand inspection, one of the measures in the war against rustlers*

secure in the knowledge that the cows he has spotted are pasturing far from the ranch headquarters, can open a gate or, with a pair of pliers, cut the fence. A cattle truck equipped with a portable loading chute can be pulled into the pasture where the cattle are rounded up and loaded in pretty short order. With the cows safely in the rig, the rustlers can be 200 miles long gone before dawn.

A successful 'rustle' requires collusion. Small meat-packing houses scattered throughout the country can make an ideal fence. With all the laws, the cowman has little defense against the criminal and practically never any recourse. He can write it off as a tax loss, but that's a pretty poor way of making a profit in the cattle business.

If a stockman's calves, or any cattle for that matter, are to be sold out of state, a health certificate must also be secured. A veterinarian must make his inspection, attesting to the fact that the animals are visibly free from sickness and have been inoculated against such dread disease as brucellosis or undulant fever, commonly referred to as Bangs. Some states have pretty strict laws prohibiting the importation of unhealthy animals.

No longer are cattle driven to market. Rather, monstrous semi-trailer trucks are backed into the cattle ramps by skillful drivers. The cowboys push and prod the calves into these huge latticed trailers, carefully counting each one as it struggles into the frightening, unknown conveyance.

In most instances calves are shipped to public auctions. Formerly, these were held at the great cattle centers such as Kansas City, Fort Worth, Chicago and Denver. More recently, however, cattle auctions have moved to the country, partly to be closer to the feed lots, partly because many of the packing houses have left the cities, likewise dispersing themselves to be nearer the feeders.

The buyers at the auctions are generally the operators of the feed lots. Here, in great pens, the cattle are fattened from 120 to as much as 360 days, readying them for slaughter. Feeders endeavor to purchase calves they predict will fatten quickly and efficiently. Calves are sold to the highest bidder. If the market is high, say forty-five to fifty cents per pound, the rancher will have a good year. If the market is low at twenty-eight to thirty-one cents, the stockman may find that his year's operation has left him in the red. The cow-calf operator

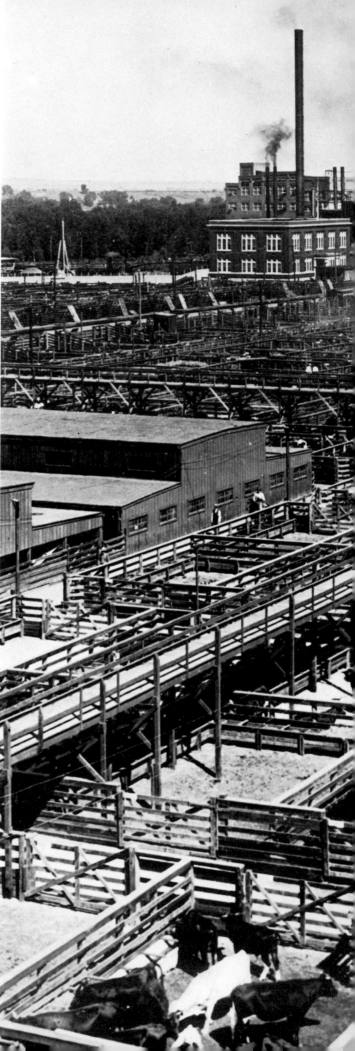

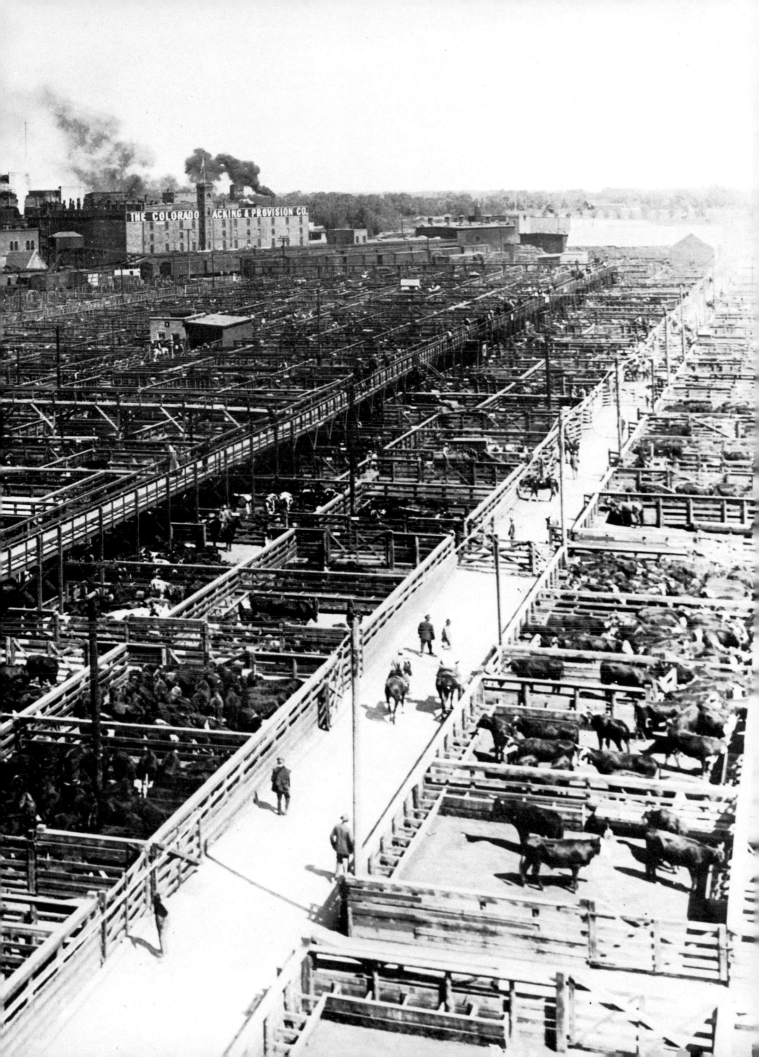

Scenes at two Colorado cattle auctions. These sales are generally held on a weekly basis. The auctioneer's chant is so rapid that the words are indistinguishable to an untrained ear

has practically no control over what his calves will bring. At best he can gamble on the market, hoping either that by holding off a little longer prices will rise or guessing that the market is at its top and selling now. It's really less work and more fun to lose money at Las Vegas.

The auction house is like a small semi-circular arena ringed by a grandstand with seats or benches facing the pit below. Here, on a sawdust-covered floor, the cattle are shown, having been brought in from the pens outside the building. Above the pit, facing the grandstand, secure behind a sturdy podium, sit the auctioneer and clerk. These officials nearly always wear white hats, a sign of integrity.

There is a sense of suspense about a cattle auction. The sellers wonder what they'll receive; the buyer wonders what he'll have to pay. The calves, ideally in bunches of twenty, referred to as carload lots, are pushed into the ring where the

ring-man prods the animals around with a yellow cane so the buyers can get a view of the stock. As each lot is about to be auctioned, the auctioneer gets a price from the ring-man, the lowest figure at which he thinks the bidding should start. The hawker knows the local market, the auctioneer knows auctioneering.

'Hey, hey, boys,' barks the auctioneer in a falsetto voice. 'Looky here, looky here, steer calves from the Lone Star Ranch, top quality, high country, good stuff. Now who'll give me thirty-four, thirty-four, thirty-four a pound?'

'Thirty-four, thirty-four,' rasps the auctioneer in his singsong cry. 'Now thirty-five, I've got thirty-five, thirty-five, do I hear thirty-six cents?'

And so it goes. Up at first by pennies, then by half cents, finally by less until the auctioneer finally pleads, 'I got thirty-eight and a quarter. Do I hear a half, who'll give me a half, a half, a half?' Bang goes the gavel. 'Sold, sold for thirty-eight and a quarter to Killmore Feed Lots.' The calves are then pushed out of the ring and onto a set of scales. Here they are weighed and the total price calculated almost instantly. And only at that moment does the stockman, watching his calves disappear from the ring, never to see them again, leave his seat in the stands to pick up his check for a year's work. It may be a moment of joy or despair.

After the fall sale, the rancher's year begins again. This is the time to test the cows to determine how many are with calf. Pregnancy testing requires each cow to be brought into the squeeze and physically examined. An experienced cowboy can detect a fetus as early as the fourth month, but to become proficient a man must have tested several thousand cows.

Those cows found to be pregnant are placed in one pen, while the 'empties' are separated in another. A pragmatic stockman, irrespective of the quality of a cow which has not conceived, will dispose of that animal at auction. He knows that such a cow is either unreliable or possibly infertile and that by keeping her over for another breeding season, considering the cost of feed, she will prove to be nothing but a liability.

While the cow is in the squeeze is a good opportunity to check her age. This the cowboy does by prying open her mouth with a metal jaw-spreader. Teeth worn flat to the gums indicate age, but not necessarily old age. Teeth become worn from grit and sand in the grass. However, a cow without teeth cannot get enough to eat, she becomes gaunt, her milk supply diminishes and her calf starves. In most cases, 'gummers' are sent to market as 'cutters,' the lowest grade of beef.

On the other hand, if a cow has a superior record for producing excellent calves, the stockman may decide to fit her with a set of false teeth. Now, with her mouth pried open, is the time to clip in the metal dentures. False teeth can add a couple of years to a cow's productive life.

Today's rancher is a businessman in work-clothes, a laborer, often with a college education. He's a gambling man, with the elements and the market his unpredictable odds. And perhaps most significant, he is a man with a fierce affection for his animals—his horse and his cows.

Keeping a ranch going, with the one purpose supplying the consumer with good beef—at a profit to be sure—demands much energy and considerable devotion. It is all summed up in this little ditty a cowman once wrote:

'Pity not the lonesome cowboy,
His best friend is his horse.
He's got empty cows and dry grass
And his banker, of course.'

Playing the Cowboy

The wonders of the West, with its vast ranges, its majestic mountains, its intrepid men, have long lured many an Easterner to become a part of its drama. Some have played a major role, others only a minor part. There have been many acts and many actors, both genuine and fraudulent.

Most amusing and entertaining to the cowboys were those men who came West and were dubbed the 'dudes.' In the early days the term dude was applied to the 'city slickers,' Easterners seeking their fortunes in less rough-and-ready occupations than that of punching cows. To the cowboy, these men, in their prim clothes and proper manners were a laughingstock. And the cowboy, in a bullying sort of way, took advantage of them.

By the turn of the century some farseeing stockmen observed the number of hunters and vacationers drawn to the West. They also saw, in this influx of urbanites trying to get away from their humdrum lives, the dollar sign.

Men with ranches in the wilds opened their headquarters as hunting lodges. Advertising a plentiful supply of big game—elk and bear, antelope or moose—the more hardy Easterners wearing ten-gallon hats and high-heeled boots ventured forth in search of a 'he-man' experience and a 'head' to adorn their libraries, dens or trophy rooms. The rancher supplied, at a cost-plus-profit basis, accommodation, often pretty plush, pack-horses, and real wranglers who made camp, did the cooking, and dressed out the kill. On most of these so-called hunting expeditions the guest was led right to the quarry; his greatest effort was to pull the trigger. This still goes on today. All in all, it's great for the ego development of certain temperaments, as well as an effective method of driving ecologists up the walls, by ridding the earth of a lot of useless wild animals.

Other stockmen opened their home ranches to vacationers, men and women who had money and time enough to spend two or three weeks in the 'Wild West,' absorbing by osmosis something of its 'gutsy' flavor.

Today dude ranching is a lucrative business. The right costume helps one to get into the spirit— cowboy boots, tight levis, a silk shirt and a big Stetson hat can instantly transform any New Yorker into a genuine 'soda water' cowboy. Here the Easterner can 'sit a horse,' ride among the cows and exuberate on a mountain-pack trip, eating beans from a pie plate and drinking coffee from a tin cup. Around the night campfire, a cowboy will sing a doleful song accompanied by a twanging guitar. Here the dude can indulge in fantasy, imagining himself camped on the lone prairie surrounded by lowing cattle, on the alert for an Indian attack. Playing cowboy this way is pretty thrilling, entirely romantic and completely safe.

On the other hand, playing cowboy in the present-day rodeo circuit is an entirely different game. This is gambling for pretty high stakes and a mistake can mean losing for keeps.

Rodeo, Spanish for 'roundup,' began long ago, but no one can quite agree when or where. Most likely, after a roundup when the cowboys gathered from two or three ranches, some buster decided just for fun to see who could sit a bucking bronc the longest, who could stay aboard a pitching bull without getting dumped. Men, skilled in roping a steer, competed for the honor of being the quickest at roping, throwing and tying a little critter all set for branding.

At these early rodeos the only spectators were the ranch-hands themselves, the only contestants the outfit's cowboys. The fence making up the corral was the grandstand and the whiskey bottle was the refreshment. It was all very informal, all terribly rough.

Today the cowboys are professionals. Urbanite spectators fill grandstands designed for thousands.

A hard way to make money

Below: *At a South Dakota rodeo the chute opens and a bull explodes into the arena.* Right: *'Rodeo queens', cowgirls of the 1920s who performed riding and roping tricks and rode bucking broncs as well*

Pop is the standard liquid refreshment and food is also served in the form of a hot dog snug in a bun and doused with mustard.

The modern rodeo is a well-organized athletic event drawing contestants from all parts of the country and spectators by the droves. The Rodeo Cowboys Association has set out pretty rigid rules which the cowboys have to observe, partly to ensure that the contestants will be competing on an equal basis, but also to safeguard the cowboys and the animals.

At the big rodeos, with the stands filled to bursting, the announcer in a voice as silvery as his Stetson hat, calls over the PA system:

'Ladies and gentlemen, you are about to witness one of the great spectaculars of the West. Here the finest cowboys in America pit their skill and daring against untamed and dangerous animals.

'Each of these men has paid a fee just to enter this contest. This entitles him to compete for the prize money. That's all he'll get out of it—nothing more but your applause. So give them a big hand.

'And here they come—the Grand Entry—I give you, ladies and gentlemen, the Annual Western Rodeo!'

The grand entry at a rodeo is often a parade on horseback run at breakneck speed around the arena. Generally it's led by a 'Queen' and her shapely female attendants, trailed by the cowboys whose gait seems more casual. The cowgirls follow, in tight, iridescent pants of pale green, lavender or blue, often with matching shirts and hats.

Already the band has sounded a frantic march as the horsemen tear around. When the entire group has circled the grounds, the Queen pulls her mount to a staggering halt before the grandstand. Now the band strikes up, the flag waves proudly, the spectators stand, the men hold their hats over their chests, and all sing the National Anthem. The show has begun.

The bareback bull-riders may be first to burst from the gates. Here the cowboy must stay on a writhing, twisting, bucking, grunting 2,000-pound beast for at least eight seconds if he is to score. And the points he makes depend not only upon his skill, but equally on the viciousness of the bull. In other

words, both animal and rider are rated, the bull on a scale of twenty-five. A mild-mannered bull can pull a man's score down, no matter how able he is. Nor do the cowboys choose the beasts they are to ride, for these are drawn for them by the judges.

A noisy buzzer sounds when the eight seconds are up. The rider who has managed to stay on now tries to jump clear. It is at this moment that the clowns, employed specially to distract the bull from the staggering or fallen cowboy, begin their dangerous task. Carrying brooms, and a red rubber barrel, large enough for one of them to climb inside to hide, the clowns taunt the bull in all manner of ways. Often, amidst the shrieks of the crowd, the bull charges the barrel, rolling it hither and yon, meanwhile giving the bull-rider time to escape.

Bull-riding is considered one of the most dangerous of rodeo events and it takes a cowboy with raw courage and steel guts to excel.

Said Bill Nelson, the 1971 bull-riding champion, 'My horses run off with me and I can't ride my bulls.' It was that sort of modesty, however, that won Nelson $21,000!

The rodeo events are frequently interspersed with special acts. The trick roper spinning and twirling his long lariat, jumping in and out of the big loops, is a favorite. Girls in pink pants more form-fitting than a kid glove, straddling a pair of

Above: *Steer wrestling, sometimes referred to as 'bulldogging'*

Below: *The object of bulldogging is to wrench the steer to the ground, a none too simple feat*

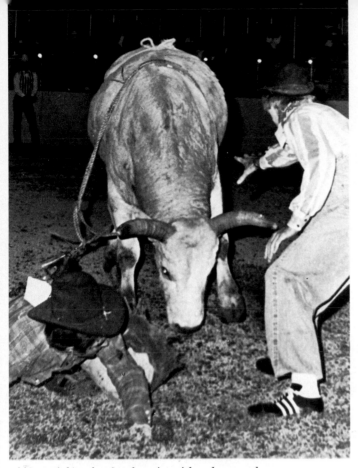

Above right: *Another favorite with rodeo crowds
is calf roping.* Above: *The rodeo clown whose
function it is to keep the crowd amused and who
sometimes saves a cowboy from grief*

beautifully trained horses which gallop through a
ring of fire, also add excitement and glamor to the
circus flavor of the show.

But the real cowboy events are the bull-riding
and calf-roping, the steer-wrestling, 'bull-dogging'
and bronc-riding. That's what the crowd pays to
see.

Calf-roping is a contest of perfect teamwork
between a cowboy and his horse versus a runaway
calf. The rider must wait behind a rope barrier
until the calf is released. Then racing behind, the
cowboy loops his rope over the fleeing calf's neck.
Suddenly, the well-trained cow pony stops short,
so that the rope, looped around the saddle horn, is
kept taut, allowing the rider to dismount and run
along the rope to grab the struggling calf and throw
him. The cowboy may either pick up the calf and
throw it on its side—called 'flanking'—or wrench
the calf to the earth by pulling on its foreleg—
referred to as 'legging.' Now the roper must tie
three legs securely with a 'piggin string,' a short
length of rope which many cowboys carry in
readiness in their mouths. A good man can rope
and tie his calf in fifteen seconds, but the record
time, seven and a half seconds, was set in 1967 by

Junior Garrison, twice world champion.

Phil Lyne of George West, Texas, the 1971
calf-roping champion, earned himself over $28,000
by his consistent speed.

Steer-wrestling requires brains and brawn and
bravery. Here, chasing at a gallop a running steer,
the cowboy must spring from his horse to grab for
the horns. Locking them in his arms, with legs
outstretched and high heels acting as a brake, he
must wrench and twist the steer's head, throwing
the animal to the ground. To score, all four feet and
head must point in the same direction. The only
help a steer wrestler gets is from a 'hazer,' a man
who rides to the side of the running steer to keep it
from veering away from the wrestler.

There's money in steer wrestling for the winners.
Billy Hale of Oklahoma, the 1971 champion,
pocketed $23,000 for his skill. Some of his steers
he threw in just over five seconds. Steve Gramith
toppled one in three and seven-tenths seconds to
set a National Finals Rodeo record in 1971.

Probably the most spectacular act, the one event
that sums up in the popular imagination what a
Western rodeo is all about, is the bareback bronc-
riding. Mounted on an untamed, cantankerous

Two cowboys riding bareback. The one on the left still has his center of gravity over the horse, but the one on the right may hit the ground before his pony does

mass of wild horsemeat, whose single idea is to get rid of anything on his back, the cowboy starts out somewhat disadvantaged. With nothing more to hang onto than a bit of rigging about the size of a suitcase handle, the rider explodes from the chute on an animal that packs the punch of dynamite. As the horse bucks and twists, twirls and lunges, the bronco-buster flays his legs, spurring the animal's shoulders and waving his free hand, for it is against the rules to touch the horse. For eight seconds the rider must stay aboard the bucking hunk of horseflesh if he is to win any points at all. Many a cowboy is dumped long before the time expires and acquires nothing but experience and some broken bones; others who may survive collect only a few points due to an infraction of the rules or the bad luck of drawing a mild bronco.

Despite the difficulties and disappointments associated with bareback riding, the rewards are tempting. Joe Alexander, the 1971 champion, earned over $28,000 for the pounding he took.

The rodeo circuit is a grueling one, yet if a cowboy is to earn any money he must be willing to enter contest after contest. Rodeos are now held in all parts of the country, from San Francisco to New York City's Madison Square Garden.

Some cowboys literally live out of their suitcases, several flying their own planes to get from city to city, for that's where the money is. Not only are these men superb athletes, but many have other interests too. Among them are men who operate cattle ranches, one's a TV and movie actor, one's a veterinarian and another a professional football player. Some train and shoe horses, some operate night clubs, and at least one paints pictures for a hobby.

Cowboying has not been the province of men alone. Women have many times taken an active part not only in the work of branding and steering, but as early as the 1920s joined the ranks of rodeo contestants as bronco-busters and calf ropers. Today, however, women compete in a special event called 'barrel-racing.' Here three barrels are set up in a triangular pattern as markers. The cowgirls race their fast ponies against time around

If the rodeo contestant excels at this sort of thing to the point where he carries off the prize, it might be something like this ornately tooled and silver studded saddle (right). The bull's horn chair can provide seating of an entirely different sort, strictly for relaxation

the markers, losing points if their horses tip one over. All dressed up in the fanciest of Western duds, these spunky girls really produce cheers from the crowd.

While rodeoing is without exception one of the roughest, toughest and grubbiest sports in America, it is also the cleanest one. Since each man competes as an individual against himself, gambling interests have little if any leverage. There are no rodeo teams, no Fort Worth Bronco-busters nor Cheyenne Cowpokes. The cowboy is independent, he cannot be bought and sold by a company of

GANO-DOWNS

NATIONAL WESTERN
HORSE SHOW RODEO

investors. He will not bargain, nor can he become enslaved. True, the cowboy doesn't earn what a professional football player can make, but neither is he beholden to a salaried coach or trainer. The cowboy is his own coach, his own trainer. He's not for hire and he can't be fired. He's his own manager, his own employer. As such, he's one of the most respected athletes in the nation.

So profoundly has the cowboy captured the popular imagination that a special museum, the Cowboy Hall of Fame, has been established in his honor at Oklahoma City, the capital of Oklahoma. Here one can see trophies won by the champions, huge paintings and great sculpture pertaining to cowboys and the life of the West.

The renown of the cowboy, however, has spread much farther than the halls of a museum in Oklahoma. Long before the idea of a monument paying tribute to the lonely, winsome character known as the cowboy was ever conceived, his charisma had already reached the remote corners of the world. It came about in a variety of marvelous ways.

Frederick Remington, a stocky, nineteen-year-old football player, studied art at Yale. His father's premature death, however, forced the young man not only to give up college, but to fulfill an over-riding ambition to go West. Beginning in 1881, young Remington studied the West and its characters. In 1886 he published his first illustration, 'Indian Scouts,' in *Harper's Weekly*.

Charles Russell was sixteen years old when his father, in 1880, finally gave in to his artistic son's lopsided desire to go West. Charlie started work on a Montana sheep ranch and got tired. Next he found work with a hunter and trapper, Jake

In the early 1900s the fun sometimes got a little lively around the saloons. Charles M. Russell could have made this drawing from life, as was certainly the case with the sculpture (left), *a self-portrait*

Dance! you short-horn dance!

Hoover, and began sketching wildlife. Later he got
a job wrangling horses and thereafter worked as a
cowboy on several big spreads, all the time making
pictures to give his friends. It wasn't until 1880
that *Harper's Weekly* published his picture 'Caught
in the Act.' But from then on Charlie Russell was
on the way to becoming the first cowboy artist of
America.

In good measure, it was the dramatic credibility
and the untiring labors of Frederick Remington
and Charles Russell that brought the romance of
the West to the parlors of the East. In addition to
the pictures these men were producing, there were
also writers who knew the cowboy and his way of
life.

Owen Wister, a Philadelphian who made several
trips to the West for his health, wrote in 1902 a
best-selling novel, *The Virginian*. This book,
together with Zane Grey's fanciful stories, the most
famous of which was *Riders of the Purple Sage* in
1912, so enthralled the eastern readers that the
West and its cowboys became overnight a land of
majesty and heroes.

If Charlie Russell was the cowboy artist, then
Will James was the cowboy author. His poignant
story *Smoky*, illustrated by the author, is a master-
piece of cowboy understatement. Nor can *Cowboy*
by Ross Santee be surpassed as the gentle tale of
a real cowpuncher's wistful life.

Without question, the most unforgettable and
beloved cowboy character on the American scene
was Will Rogers. Raised on his father's ranch in
Oklahoma, Will worked on the famous 101 Spread,
which among other things ran a Wild West show.
Here he was taught much of his cowboying by Bill
Pickett, the half-black, half-Choctaw Indian cowboy who invented 'bulldogging.' What made Will
Rogers famous was not his cowpunching abilities,
but his finesse with rope tricks and his homespun
humor.

It was his custom on stage, while twirling his
lariat in complicated convolutions, to comment in
his western drawl upon the politics of the day, and
his observations were telling:

'A flock of Democrats will replace a mess of

Republicans. It won't mean a thing. They'll go in like all the rest of them. Go in on promises and come out on alibis.'

If pictures and books, Wild West shows and humorists dramatized the West at the turn of the century, motion pictures brought it all to life. In 1916 the celluloid hero of the day was William S. Hart, only to be eclipsed in the 1930s by a more up-to-date version, Tom Mix. While it was inconceivable that any actor could surpass the portrayals of these taciturn, brave, honest cowboys, there later appeared on the screen much like a silent comet illuminating the sky, the epitome of the folk-hero, Gary Cooper. It's been said of cowboys that they are men of few words and Cooper proved it. Some joker observed that the longest sentence Cooper ever spoke on a film was, 'You're fired!' And yet it was just such lengthy dialogue that won him the affection and respect of millions.

There seems to be no end to the persistency of the cowboy as a hero. For a long time Hollywood has been in the business of building all sorts of valorous men, but among its most recent successes has been the making of John Wayne. Here is the stoic Westerner personified, the he-man plus. Here on the silver screen in full technicolor is the living example of Owen Wister's *Virginian*, who speaking right before your eyes says, 'When you call me that, smile!' What is more, John Wayne has been not only the making of Hollywood, but an ego-builder for a nation. His sincerity, his belief in the worthwhile value of the cowboy as an individualist, as a man devoted to the cause of right against wrong, strength against weakness, have won him millions of fans wherever movies are shown. His is a wonderful world of stark contrasts, with no shades of gray, where the good guys wear white hats and always win. While no one ever lived nor ever will live in so simplistic a never-never land, it is certainly the sort of world many people dream of. John Wayne fulfills that will-o'-the-wisp hope.

For all their skill or glamor or romantic appeal, it is not the writer, artist, humorist or movie idol who made the cowboys; it is the cowboys who made them. And it's happening this very day. Somewhere on the vast range country of America there is a cowpuncher climbing a windmill, branding a calf, steering a little critter, maybe even pulling an old cow out of a mudhole.

As long as thrifty and critical housewives buy hamburger, as long as fine restaurants serve tender and high-priced sirloins, there will be the cowboy. Some may cut out cows on a motorcycle or jeep, some may even check their cattle in an airplane, but on many, many an up-to-date ranch, there is still no substitute for the cowboy and his horse.

There's a saying that if something is natural and right and fitting, it's 'as American as apple pie.' Not everyone can or wants to bake an apple pie and not everyone can or wants to become a cowboy. But it's fair to say that in the minds of many men, even if only for fleeting moments, there's a hankering to be as free and rugged, as engaging and boisterous, as hardworking, daring and independent, as truly American, as the cowboy.

Charles M. Russell's The Virginian. *He rolled
his own*

Further Reading

Trail Driving Days by Dee Brown, Scribner, 1952.
Before Barbed Wire by Mark Brown and W. Felton, Holt, 1956.
The Longhorns by J. Frank Dobie, Grosset and Dunlap, 1957.
Riders of the Purple Sage by Zane Grey, Grosset and Dunlap.
Wild Cow Tales by Ben Green, Knopf, 1969.
I and Tex by Royal B. Hassrick, Vantage Press, 1946.
The Story of the Cowboy by E. Hough, Gregg, 1970.

Smoky by Will James, Scribner, 1926.
The Cattlemen by Marie Sandoz, Hastings, 1958.
Cowboy by Ross Santee, Hastings, 1964.
A Texas Cowboy by Charles A. Siringo, Bison, 1966.
The Cowboy at Work by Fay E. Ward, Hastings, 1958.
The Trembling Herd by Paul I. Wellman, Carrick & Evans, 1939.
The Virginian by Owen Wister, Macmillan, 1925.
Cowboys and Cattle Country by Don Ward & J. C. Dykes. Harper and Row, 1961.

Acknowledgments

This book owes its completion to the generous assistance of many people. Included are Mr. Terry Magnin of the Colorado State Museum, Mrs. Alys Freeze, Mrs. Kay Kane, Mrs. Opal Harber, Mrs. Hazel Lundberg, Mrs. Brenda McClurkin, Miss Marion Spann Morriss and Mrs. James H. Davis of the Denver Public Library; Mr. Forrest Basford and Mr. E. C. Larkin and Mrs. Christine Anderson of the Western Livestock Journal; Mr. Robert S. Crook of the Colorado Cattleman's Association; Mr. John Benson and Mr. Roger Sherman of the Leo Burnet Company; Mr. Owen Smith of Oak Hill, Virginia; Mr. Randy Witt of the Rodeo Cowboy's Association; to Barbara Morgan Hassrick for typing and editorial advice; and to every cowpuncher and cattleman who has ever worked with the author as a rancher to give the book whatever flavor of the cowboy's life this work may contain.

The quote from Will Rogers on page 136 is reproduced by courtesy of the Will Rogers' Memorial Commission.

The author and publishers would like to thank the following individuals and organizations who supplied the illustrations for this book.

Amon Carter Museum : Pages 23, 31 (top), 48, 53, 66 (top), 67 (top and bottom), 74, 78–79, 134, 135, 136–137, 138, 140. *Philip Anschutz Collection* : Pages 60–61. *Barnaby's Picture Library* : Pages 6–7 (top and bottom), 8–9, 12 (top), 14 (top and bottom). *S. O. Butcher Collection* : Page 55 (bottom). *Camera Press, London* : Page 125 (bottom). *Colorado Cattleman's Association* : Page 88 (top). *Darol Dickinson, Calhan, Colorado* : Pages 75 (top), 106 (bottom), 107, jacket flap. *Denver Art Museum* : Pages 26, 27, 39 (bottom). *Denver Public Library* : Pages 4–5, 24–25, 33 (top), 35 (top), 40 (top), 42 (bottom), 46 (top), 47, 49 (top and bottom), 52, 54 (top and bottom), 55 (top), 62, 63, 69, 72 (top and bottom), 73, 76, 77 (top), 80 (left), 84–85, 89 (top), 92 (bottom), 96 (top), 100 (top), 102 (bottom), 104 (top and bottom), 105, 109 (top), 112–113, 116 (top and bottom), 121, 126 (bottom), 133. *Denver Union Corporation* : Pages 114–115. *Mary Evans' Picture Library* : Pages 8 (bottom), 12 (bottom), 13 (top and bottom), 16 (top and bottom), 17 (top and bottom), 18 (bottom), 20, 21. *Phil Fahs Photo* : Pages 100 (bottom), 102 (top), 106 (top), 115 (bottom right). *Gilcrease Institute of American History and Art* : Page 39 (top). *W. L. Hamilton, Z.E.F.A.* : Pages 119, 123, jacket flap. *Historical Society of New Mexico* : Page 58 (bottom). *Mack Jones* : Pages 70 (top), 84 (bottom), 93. *Kansas State Historical Society* : Front endpapers. *King Ranch, Kingsville/Western Livestock Journal* : Page 83. *Ruth Koerner Oliver* : Pages 64–65. *Municipal Art Department, City of Los Angeles* : Page 96 (bottom). *National Western Stock Show* : Pages 88 (bottom), 89 (bottom), 92 (top). *North American Limousin Foundation* : Page 84 (center). *Old Lincoln County Memorial Commission* : Page 58 (top). *Kipp Parker Photo* : Page 111. *Pictorial Press/John R. Hamilton-Globe* : Page 19 (top). *Picturepoint, London* : Pages 131 (bottom), 132. *M. Pitner, Z.E.F.A.* : Page 122. *Rodeo Information Foundation* : Pages 124, 126 (top), 127 (left and right), 129. *Fred Rosenstock Gallery* : Pages 40 (center), 45, 66 (bottom). *Lemon Saks Gallery* : Pages 98–99. *Taken from THE 1902 EDITION OF THE SEARS, ROEBUCK CATALOGUE.* © 1969 by Crown Publishers, Inc. Used by permission of Crown Publishers, Inc.: Pages 77 (above), 80 (top, center, below right). *Jerry Sinise Photo* : Pages 84 (top), 86, 91, 101 (top and bottom), 103, 109 (bottom), 112 (bottom). *State Historical Society of Colorado* : Pages 32 (top), 36–37 (top), 36 (bottom), 42 (top), 46 (bottom), 70 (bottom), 75 (bottom). *Walker Art Studio* : Pages 94–95, 106 (center). *Warner Bros* : Pages 10–11, 15, 18 (top). *Martin Weaver/Susan Griggs* : Page 110. *Western Americana* : Pages 28 (top), 29, 30 (top left, bottom, top right), 31 (bottom), 37 (bottom), 38 (bottom), 41, 51, 56 (top), 80 (below left), 120, 128, 130, back endpapers. *W. F. Whitfield* : Page 59 (right). *Adam Woolfitt/Susan Griggs* : Pages 2–3, 40 (top), 125 (top), 131 (top and center). *Wyoming State Archives and Historical Department* : Page 56 (bottom).

Index